GEMINI

22 MAY – 21 JUNE

First published in Great Britain 2013
by Mills & Boon, an imprint of Harlequin (UK) Limited,
Eton House, 18-24 Paradise Road, Richmond, Surrey TW9 1SR

HOROSCOPES 2014 © Dadhichi Toth 2013

ISBN: 978 0 263 91096 4

Cover design by Anna Viniero
Typeset by Midland Typesetters

Harlequin (UK) policy is to use papers that are natural, renewable and recyclable products and made from wood grown in sustainable forests. The logging and manufacturing processes conform to the legal environmental regulations of the country of origin.

Printed and bound in Spain
by Blackprint CPI, Barcelona

Dedicated to

The Light of Intuition

Sri V. Krishnaswamy—mentor and friend

Special thanks to

Nyle Cruz for her tireless support and suggestions

Thanks to

Joram and Isaac for hanging in there

Additional appreciation to

Devika Adlakha for her excellent editorial support

ABOUT DADHICHI

Dadhichi is one of Australia's foremost astrologers and is frequently seen on television and in other media. He has the unique ability to draw from complex astrological theory to provide clear, easily understandable advice and insights for people who want to know what their futures may hold.

In the 29 years that Dadhichi has been practising astrology, face reading and other esoteric studies, he has conducted over 10,000 consultations. His clients include celebrities, political and diplomatic figures, and media and corporate identities from all over the world.

Dadhichi's unique blend of astrology and face reading helps people fulfill their true potential. His extensive experience practising Western astrology is complemented by his research into the theory and practice of Eastern forms of astrology.

Dadhichi has been a guest on many Australian television shows, and several of his political and worldwide forecasts have proved uncannily accurate. He appears regularly on Australian television networks and is a columnist for online and offline Australian publications.

His websites—www.astrology.com.au and www.facereader.com— attract hundreds of thousands of visitors each month and offer a wide variety of features, helpful information and services.

MESSAGE FROM
❧ DADHICHI ❧

Hello once again and welcome to your 2014 horoscope!

Time and Speed are the governors of our lives these days. There's *never enough* time, and the hectic pace at which we move is getting *too much* to handle. So we oscillate between never enough and too much. We are either too slow in finishing our tasks, or the hands of the clock appear to be whizzing forward, especially when we're under pressure. We are constantly trying to create more time just to keep up with everyone else. And all those people are rushing out of control. What is this madness? We need to reclaim control of our lives and bring these terrible twins of speed and time under our control if we are ever to master our destinies.

According to Einstein and his incredible theory of relativity, speed and time are related. The faster we move, the quicker time flies. As we crank up the pace of our lives, time is impacted upon even more. You don't need me to tell you that; your experience will remind you of this fact every day, especially when you look in the mirror and see an additional wrinkle or two from time to time. Age is the favourite child of these two parents: speed and time. In the old days, it used to be the elderly who complained about the pace of time. But now, everyone, even youngsters, grumble about how little time they have and how they are forever trying to cram as much fun and experience into the moment. This attitude seems to be the order of the day, yet it will never, ever be enough.

The planets also operate on the same principle of speed and time, and this is how we generate astrological forecasts. Speed is related to the distance these planets traverse around the Sun, and the time it takes for them to do their celestial dance around the Sun is referred to as a planetary cycle.

We often talk about being in harmony with our environment and leaving as invisible a carbon footprint as we can, thus re-establishing natural equilibrium on earth. But our larger celestial environment is something we've overlooked. Ancient astrologers, however, knew the secret of our interconnectedness to the greater environment, and they gave us esoteric spiritual techniques for tuning in to these controllers of our fate. But how do you control the planets, let alone speed and time? It is through intuition, perception and self-awareness. By developing your perception and intuitive faculties, you will be one of the survivors in this brave new world.

If you're up to the challenge, this will increase your psychic abilities, thereby helping you surmount the obstacles of speed and time. You will bring yourself into harmony with your own physical, mental and emotional needs, and you will be able to tune easily in to your environment and fellow man. You will sense what these planetary energies are doing to you and can adjust yourself accordingly. This requires the subtle art of spiritual listening. This is not the hearing that is done with your ears. This is listening done with the heart. Through these simple techniques you *will* conquer time!

Our frames of reference are changing, and our ability to adapt to the light-speed pace is demanding refinements and adjustments in perception. In 2014, take the time to move at your own pace and look at what it is *you* want to achieve, not what is foisted upon you by culture, family and the establishment. Run your own race, and even if you are moving in high gear, at least you will be the one in control, not the clock. Use the transits and forecasts in the last chapter to help you gain an overview of the likely time of events. By taking control of your time and slowing the pace of life, you begin to control your destiny. In doing so, you rediscover the pleasure of your own self and the talents that you have been endowed with. This will then be a time of self-empowerment and great fulfilment.

Your astrologer,

Dadhichi Toth

CONTENTS

CONTENTS
CONTINUED

CONTENTS
CONTINUED

GEMINI
PROFILE

YOUR DAILY LIFE IS YOUR TEMPLE
AND YOUR RELIGION.

Kahlil Gibran

GEMINI SNAPSHOT

Key Life Phrase		I Think
Zodiac Totem		The Twins
Zodiac Symbol	♊	
Zodiac Facts		Third sign of the zodiac; mutable, barren, positive, masculine and airy
Zodiac Element		Air
Key Characteristics		Multi-talented, a thinker, talkative, social, scattered, has diverse interests, loves variety and excitement
Compatible Star Signs		Gemini, Cancer, Leo, Libra, Aquarius, Aries and Taurus

Mismatched Signs		Virgo, Sagittarius, Pisces, Scorpio and Capricorn
Ruling Planet		Mercury
Love Planets		Venus and Jupiter
Finance Planet		Moon
Speculation Planet		Venus
Career Planets		Neptune, Jupiter and Mars
Spiritual and Karmic Planets		Venus and Saturn
Destiny Planet		Venus
Friendship Planet		Mars
Famous Geminis		Colin Farrell, Marilyn Monroe, Johnny Depp, Clint Eastwood, Paula Abdul, Kylie Minogue, Morgan Freeman, Mike Myers, Paul McCartney, Russell Brand, Elizabeth Hurley, Bob Dylan, Drew Carey, Lenny Kravitz, Heidi Klum, Courteney Cox, Natalie Portman, Angelina Jolie and Nicole Kidman
Lucky Numbers and Significant Years		5, 6, 8, 14, 15, 17, 23, 24, 26, 32, 33, 35, 41, 42, 44, 50, 51, 53, 68, 77 and 86

Lucky Gems	Emerald, peridot, diamond, quartz crystal, aquamarine and jade
Lucky Fragrances	Basil, sandalwood, thyme, peppermint and lavender
Affirmation/Mantra	I am calm.
Lucky Days	Wednesday, Friday and Saturday

❧ GEMINI OVERVIEW ❧

❝ IT'S BETTER TO BE HATED FOR WHAT YOU ARE
THAN TO BE LOVED FOR WHAT YOU'RE NOT. ❞

MARILYN MONROE

Geminis have amazing minds, and people are fascinated by the way you can switch from one thing to another without missing a beat. Your interests are so diverse that sometimes it may seem that you are superficial for taking a bit of this and a bit of that and bringing them together as a wonderful idea.

The downside of this remarkable gathering of ideas is that you overtax your wonderful brain and need to step back, just for a moment. Being highly strung, you run the risk of spreading yourself too thin by taking on too much and not always completing what you begin.

Gemini, you are known as the eternal student, and you don't really mind what the subject is. You just want to learn! You are quite good at assembling a multitude of facts and then turning them into your next great idea. You don't always stay with this idea to the end, but this doesn't concern you all that much. What would concern you is not having that great idea in the first place.

GREAT COMMUNICATOR

Communication is your No. 1 asset, Gemini. Your knowledge of the written and spoken word is immense. You have an incredible breadth of knowledge and can to talk to almost anyone about your different views and life experiences.

A Gemini can often be found with a pen in one hand and paper in the other. They could be writing their memoirs, researching a new project or just putting their thoughts on paper. There are many journalists, writers and advisers born under this sign; their gift for words makes a lasting impression on those who come into contact with them.

You are quick to make decisions and quite prepared to run the risk of losing an opportunity that is presented to you. You can, however, find the perfect balance between speculation and careful decision-making if you rein in your impulsiveness a little. Discipline brings great power, and it will give you the ability to use your wit and intelligence to achieve almost anything you want in life.

Geminis are energetic and clever, and people are drawn to your wonderful company. Your adaptable nature makes you interesting to others, and you can strike up a conversation on the local bus route or transatlantic flight—the place makes no difference to you.

The human mind fascinates you on many levels, and you will usually have a suitcase half packed, ready to set off on another journey. You thirst for new experiences, and it doesn't matter if it is a long or short journey, your itchy feet will set you on the path of another adventure. Again, you have to be careful not to exhaust your reserves of energy.

Mercury, your ruler, is called Kumar, or 'young person', in Indian astrology, which means that your energy and love of life will always be youthful, even in your senior years.

When things don't go to plan for you, Gemini, you tend to worry and start running around in circles. This is counterproductive, so you need to get back on track as soon as you can. Don't let others derail you from your projects as it is important that you finish what you start. You must always be master and not slave to your thought processes.

GEMINI CUSPS

ARE YOU A CUSP BABY?

Being born on the crossover of two star signs means you encompass the qualities of both. This can get tricky, and sometimes you will wonder whether you're Arthur or Martha! Some of my clients are continually mystified at whether they belong to their own star sign or the one before or after. Experiencing such feelings is nothing out of ordinary. Being born on the borderline means that you take on the qualities of both signs. The following outlines show the subtle effects of these cusp dates and how they can affect your personality.

Gemini–Taurus Cusp

If you are born during between the 22nd and the 29th of May, your adaptability is nicely offset by the rock-solid Taurus. Your combined ruling planets of Mercury and Venus will also have an impact on your character and personality.

Gemini has an insatiable curiosity, high energy levels and creative impulses, but these qualities are tempered by the security required by Taurus. This enhances your imagination and gives you the drive to succeed. Born under his combination, your chances of succeeding on a material level are greater than if you were not a cusp baby.

PATIENT AND HARD-WORKING

You are a sensitive and patient individual, and you don't mind if
success doesn't come to you immediately. You are hard-working
enough to wait for your efforts to come to fruition.

You are kind-hearted and don't hesitate to give a helping hand to anyone who needs it. You are gentle and have a practical approach to assisting others, and with your kind words and direct way of dealing with things, you get right to the heart of the problem.

You have a great work ethic and carry out the most menial of tasks with the same care and precision you would adopt for anything else you do. You are a perfectionist at heart, mainly due to the influence of Taurus. You are modest about your achievements, but the world would be a better place if you rose above your hesitancy and shared your talents with others.

Gemini–Cancer Cusp

Here we have the head and logic of Gemini and the heart and soul of Cancer. This combination gives you a more emotional and sensitive side. If you were born between the 14th and 21st of June, you will display many of the traits of the Crab, the sign of Cancer. This combination could make it difficult for you to choose between your head and your heart.

Cancer traits may also show up in a more moody Gemini who, so to speak, cannot easily separate the wheat from the chaff. This is especially so when it comes to matters of a romantic nature. It can make your sharply focused decision-making a little cloudier. This could be irritating for you, but it is a by-product of being a cusp baby.

You have strong mental traits, Gemini, but emotional issues may sometimes fog up your brain. Yoga or meditation, which will allow you to chill out regulate your breathing and let your mind and emotions settle, will help immensely. This will also create balance so that you are not swinging like a pendulum from one extreme to the other.

The important thing you need to learn, Gemini, is how to keep your brain and emotions on an even keel. Find hobbies that will stimulate your mind but keep you completely at ease and relaxed. Reading and public speaking, for instance, would be perfect for your Gemini temperament.

Cancer's connection to the Moon tends to heighten your sensitivity; don't get too upset when someone makes a thoughtless comment. You don't take kindly to criticism, even if it is constructive, and you tend to see it as an attack on your nature or intention to do the right thing by the world.

The emotional side of Cancer will give you an openness and warmth that others may try to take advantage of. You are rather perceptive when it comes to choosing friends, and your intuition is spot-on and will rarely let you down.

GEMINI CELEBRITIES

FAMOUS MALE:
JOHNNY DEPP

I've always considered Johnny Depp one of the most talented actors in Hollywood, and it should come as no surprise that he is born under the sign of Gemini. Ruled by Mercury, he is flexible, quirky and progressive, and always takes on roles that are a little unusual. Of course, Gemini prides itself on its intellectual capabilities and communicative skills, and Johnny is in possession of both!

Gemini-born individuals are restless, which is probably why Johnny dropped out of school at the age of 15. Always on the move and curious to explore the world and everything in it, he typifies the sign of Gemini. It's not a well known fact, but his versatility also extends to a love of music. Early in his career, he fronted many garage bands and even backed up Iggy Pop for one of his tours. Such is the cleverness of Gemini!

It is not often that actors can shake off the stereotypical roles that they played early in their career, but Johnny was able to do just that. The first film role that brought him wide acclaim was *Edward Scissorhands* (1990). A string of other film films followed, such as *Pirates of the Caribbean* (2003), *Finding Neverland* (2004) and *Charlie and the Chocolate Factory* (2005).

The typical Gemini is changeable by nature. Johnny once said, "I was a weird kid. I wanted to be Bruce Lee. I wanted to be on a SWAT team. When I was five, I think I wanted to be Daniel Boone." But he has used this trait to his advantage and made a successful career out of playing different characters.

FAMOUS FEMALE:
PAULA ABDUL

Paula Abdul needs no introduction as one of the world's most versatile performers. She is a high-energy singer and dancer who reinvented herself recently by appearing as a judge on eight seasons of *American Idol*.

Paula started out as a cheerleader for the Los Angeles Lakers in the early 1980s and quickly earned a reputation as a great choreographer. Soon she started working for the Jacksons and was fortunate enough to choreograph videos for Janet Jackson's album *Control*.

Paula went on to record her own songs and worked tirelessly to achieve success. Many of her singles became top ten hits, and she even won a Grammy Award for Best Video for 'Opposites Attract'. Geminis are incredibly versatile and talented, and Paula is no exception. Because Gemini rules communication of all sorts, we often find that vocalists are born under the sign of the Twins.

Paula won an Emmy for Outstanding Achievement in Choreography for *The Tracey Ullman Show* and an award for Outstanding Choreography at the 17th Annual American Music Awards. The variety and versatility that we see in her personality is also reflected in her genetic background, which is Syrian-Brazilian and French-Canadian.

GEMINI
AT LARGE

AFTER THE GAME, THE KING AND THE
PAWN GO INTO THE SAME BOX.

Italian proverb

❀ GEMINI MAN ❀

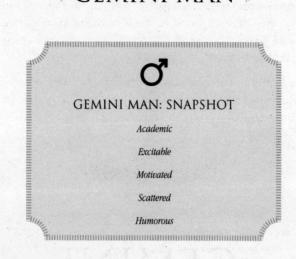

GEMINI MAN: SNAPSHOT

Academic

Excitable

Motivated

Scattered

Humorous

The Gemini male is generally tall, and if he is born in the earlier part of this star sign, he can be muscular and athletic in build. His face is usually long and proportionate, with a high forehead and thin lips.

You are always on the go, Gemini, and tend to be busier than most of your colleagues and friends. You move fast, talk fast and can sell almost anything to anyone. Doing one thing at a time doesn't necessarily appeal to you, and it is not unusual to see a Gemini male with several projects at various stages of completion.

When it comes to relationships, you can usually talk yourself out of any difficult situation. In fact, your need to talk can be quite over-whelming for a prospective romantic partner. What you need to do, Gemini, is develop your non-verbal skills so that you are not always communicating with words. Remember, less is more.

You are a loyal friend and respond with dynamic energy and speed to their needs. They can rest assured that you will always be there when they call, and this is indeed a wonderful character trait, Gemini. You are not afraid to offer advice, even when it isn't asked for, but you mean well.

The Gemini male is never satisfied with fame, reputation or money because he thinks he deserves more. If this is how you feel, you will keep searching, even if you know you will never be satisfied.

Sporty Gemini

The Gemini male usually prefers sports and physical activities to intellectual ones. You may even try to hide your insecurity about your intellect behind a façade of false bravado and macho masculinity.

You like to stand out from the crowd and take great pride in expressing your individuality, whether it is in the way you dress or speak. Ignoring you is about as useless as moving a sand hill with a teaspoon.

You don't have any trouble attracting the opposite sex, but since you are always on the lookout for change, it may make a prospective partner nervous. You love to be in love as it gives you a sense of security and the comfort of knowing that someone will be there for you.

You can be mysterious and don't reveal all of yourself at once. Your partners may even feel that they are dating two guys at once because you don't want them to get to know you too quickly. For you, it is more about the thrill of the chase than the catching of the quarry.

This is why many Gemini males prefer to play the field and may not marry until they have experienced a variety of romances, just to make sure that they have chosen 'the one'. You are a cheerful partner, with a quick wit and great intelligence. You are also a natural communicator with the ability to captivate a prospective partner's attention.

Gemini is a mutable sign, which means that you are adaptable and easily shaped by your environment. This trait will enable you to overcome adversity and adjust to the highs and lows that life throws at you. Sometimes, however, you need to pause for few moments, if that is at all possible, and think about where you are going and why. Focus is difficult, as your mind can be quite restless and scattered, but this is something you need to master.

You can be the life of the party, Gemini, as you always having a story to tell. You also have an interest in politics, philosophical ideals and other cultural and societal issues, which is why your conversation is never boring. However, you don't necessarily align yourself with the popular view and will go out on a limb with your own opinion. There is a danger, however, that you may come across as arrogant because you are well read on a subject.

You are always asking questions, Gemini, because you need to understand what is going on and why. It is from this well of information that you draw your well founded opinions, and you can certainly be proud of your intellectual achievements.

GEMINI WOMAN

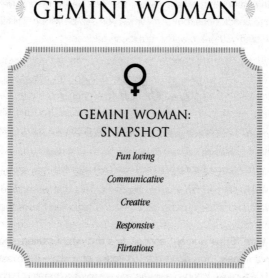

GEMINI WOMAN: SNAPSHOT

Fun loving

Communicative

Creative

Responsive

Flirtatious

The typical Gemini woman is tall, slender and very attractive. If you are born in the second half of Gemini, the slenderness may be more predominant. Those born in the first half may be slightly more curvaceous and fleshy.

Gemini, try not to become too obsessive about your looks or how others look. You also have a tendency to take great pains to hide the parts of yourself that you don't want others to see.

Your mind is deep and thoughtfully provocative. When choosing a partner, you will need someone who understands your intellectual needs, as you can be quite dismissive of anyone who is mentally lazy. They will also need to be caring, tender, romantic, reliable and well-mannered.

You are ambitious and have the fast thought processes to make things happen. However, you need to be careful not to overreact to statements that others make. You can be hypersensitive and jump to conclusions, but sometimes you can be wrong. This is not something you like to admit, but it can happen.

Gift of the Gab

You are socially very engaging and able to convey your thoughts in a way that is entertaining and witty. In fact, you have a great talent for stringing words together that make excellent sense, no matter what their origins.

The term 'Superwoman' springs to mind when talking about a Gemini female. You don't do 101 tasks of a day—it's more like 1001! You make friends easily, as you are always happy to help out, and with your brilliant time management, you are able to maintain the balance in your life.

Gemini, you probably invented multitasking and were doing it long before the concept was recognised. Your hand always shoots up at a committee meeting, and you can be relied on to start the jobs you volunteer for, even if you don't always finish them.

You are quite capable of juggling home, family and work, but you should be aware of when your fuel tank is running low, preferably before it hits empty. As your star sign regulates the nervous system, you must be careful not to skip meals. This can have a direct effect on your body and undermine your health over time. Slowing down is certainly not on your agenda, is it Gemini?

Your coffee sessions with friends are just another avenue for you to expand your mind, and you love to be with people who are interested in education, current affairs and self-improvement. It is unlikely that your social circle will include people who aren't interested in any of the topics mentioned above.

If an unsuspecting male is privy to your social circle, he will be amazed at your razor-sharp wit and lightning-fast comebacks. You are quick on the uptake, well read, and happy to chat for hours about any subject under the sun.

GEMINI CHILD

Your Gemini child is a curious creature with a well developed intellectual response to everything around them. They are inquisitive from an early age and will keep you on your toes with long lists of questions you won't have answers to.

Ruled by Mercury, your little Gemini is full of laughter, fun and practical jokes. It's a well known astrological fact that you'll never be able to shut them up. They need to let you know what they're thinking (every little detail, mind you), which helps them get rid of the nervous energy that is part of their character.

You will need to keep them busy with activities that engage their minds. This could increase your own brainpower as well, because finding games, puzzles and other activities that are challenging enough will not always be easy.

To keep your Gemini child healthy, feed them a good variety of fruits and vegetables, and lean, low-fat protein. If you do this, your Gemini child will maintain optimum levels of vitality—physically and mentally. They also have a tendency to burn calories, even if they aren't active. This is due to their nervous energy.

Clever Gemini

Gemini children are bright and excel at school, but they need to tackle one task at a time rather than skimming the surface of things.

Gemini children are full of beans and might burn themselves out, so take time to nourish them with good food, fresh air and outdoor activities. Of course, don't be swayed when they tell you that they want to stay up all night. Gemini children need adequate sleep to handle their mental overload. Problem-solving and subjects such as maths, science, communications, writing, singing and music are areas in which they shine.

As they get older and reach puberty, you need to be a step ahead of them. This is a critical time when they may overstep the bounds of their mental and physical endurance and not handle it too well. Be a friend as well as a good counsellor. This wise counsel is essential so that your Gemini child can grow into a happy, sociable, productive member of society.

GEMINI LOVER

> THE HEART HAS ITS REASONS WHICH REASON
> DOES NOT KNOW.

BLAISE PASCAL

If you are dating a Gemini, you will need to provide some stimulating conversation. If you can't do this, save yourself the time and leave now. If you are the sort of person who wants a full-on relationship after saying 'hello', then Gemini is not for you either. Geminis can appear casual in relationships, but this is because they want to develop a friendship before moving into a more serious partnership.

A Gemini lover needs to connect with someone on an intellectual level before going any further. They want a friendship to develop, and they're not afraid to ask the hard questions in an effort to establish what makes you tick. In love, Gemini may exhibit a possessive streak, but this is unusual. Boredom is a romance killer, so if you want a relationship with this star sign, you better have some witty one-liners or read up on a subject that Gemini is interested in.

 Get Tactile!

If you want to attract a Gemini, keep in mind that their erogenous zones are their hands and arms, which are ruled by the star sign of Gemini. Light touching or even massage will make them more receptive to you, and this can assist in winning their heart. At the very least it will persuade them into a more passionate mood.

At their best, Geminis can be joyful, good-natured, broadminded, experimental, radiant, friendly, enthusiastic, flexible and gentle. At their worst they are unreliable, fickle, insincere, self-focused, restless, critical and temperamental.

Geminis have a great sense of humour, which sometimes gives the impression that their conversational style is a little superficial, but this is not so. You may even think they are not interested in you, but don't judge them too quickly. This is just their way of getting to know you.

If you are a Gemini, you can be a romantic challenge to any potential mate—and a mystery as well. Your face is never blank and your expression is either lit from within or eroded by depression and moodiness. In addition to this, your emotions are always active.

Gemini natives are children of the air and they need to feel free to wander, both mentally and physically. More often than not, Gemini, you may find yourself lost and looking for the one who will fill that void in your heart.

Geminis generally marry for passionate love as well as exciting and meaningful communication. You will sweep aside the advice of older and wiser people and go where your heart takes you. Those governed by Gemini are among the lucky few who know the deep expression of being truly 'in love'.

A Gemini lover can be caring and thoughtful but will run to the hills if they feel the partnership has reached a humdrum existence. However, if they find a partnership to be whole and complete, then he or she will be the most dynamic and loyal of mates.

❦ GEMINI FRIEND ❦

Gemini, as a friend you are completely without any airs or graces. What you see is what you get. You also make people feel comfortable in any social situation.

You have the ability to listen and are a wonderful communicator. Your spontaneity is endearing, to say the least, and while it makes you unpredictable, it is this aspect of your personality that keeps others guessing.

You are outgoing, a stimulating conversationalist, and open-minded in your opinions. You love to come up with a new idea, toss it around amongst your nearest and dearest, and then watch it come to fruition. Boredom is never on your agenda, is it Gemini?

You need to guard against the tendency to gossip, as people will naturally tell you things, and it is up to you to zip your lips when you know you should. If the story doesn't seem spicy enough for you, resist the temptation to spice it up to make it more 'interesting'.

Geminis have busy social schedules and can be overwhelmed by the number of friends they have to keep in the loop. It is at these times that you need to look at the people in your circle and weed out those who are not actually friends but merely acquaintances.

If you happen to be possessive, it is not a good idea to cage your Gemini friend. They will just spread their wings like a butterfly and fly far away from you. There is no way you can tie down a Gemini, so don't waste your time.

As a Gemini friend, you will be loyal and have friends for a long time, but you are not afraid to try out new friendships. You also like to travel and will meet people from many walks of life.

As a friend, Gemini, you can be somewhat unpredictable, but underneath you are a good solid person who will go to the ends of the earth for someone who is important to you. If a friend does the wrong thing by you, however, you will let them know in no uncertain terms.

GEMINI ENEMY

ACTION MAY NOT ALWAYS BRING HAPPINESS, BUT THERE IS NO HAPPINESS WITHOUT ACTION.

WILLIAM JAMES

It is better to have Gemini as a friend than as an enemy. Geminis are wordsmiths and they will use their skills in this area as weapons of mass destruction—if the occasion arises. If you want to be on the receiving end of this vitriol, then cross a Gemini, and you will experience their venomous tongue at full force.

For the most part, Gemini, you are polite and even-tempered, but if someone upsets you, they will find out about it very quickly. You are open about your feelings and opinions, but sometimes people will take you on because they think they know better than you on a particular subject. This is not a good idea.

You will let them talk, although probably not for long, and then shoot them down with your knowledge and eloquence. You also don't like people talking behind your back. Backstabbing is not a game you enjoy, and it is one that you do not indulge in. Although you may enjoy a bit of gossip, you don't like having the tables turned on you!

GEMINI
AT HOME

ALL GREAT IDEAS ARE DANGEROUS.

Oscar Wilde

❋ HOME FRONT ❋

Gemini is the butterfly of the zodiac. They love to have space to move, change the furniture around, alter the wall colourings or swap paintings from one room to another.

Your home is a meeting place for neighbours, friends and family. Colours are likely to be aquamarine, crystal blue, violet, yellow, orange and light green. Brightness is important, too, and your home is likely to have large windows that can be thrown open for light and air. You like your furniture arranged loosely so conversations can ebb and flow. Groupings of sofas or a large table with many chairs suit your style of entertaining.

Geminis like their home environment to be neat and clean, especially the bathroom and bedroom. Your rooms will be a temple to taste and elegance, with richly patterned rugs and beautiful fabrics. Textures within your home can vary from smooth as silk to rough as stone, but they will be tastefully arranged, as is unique to Gemini. Your main aim with decorating is to have a home that is you, no matter what the latest trends may be.

You like gadgets, Gemini, and your kitchen may look like a small appliances showroom. But with your love of entertaining, there is a good chance you will use all of them. Technology fascinates you, and this is where you get your love of the latest 'must have'. Communication equipment will also be prominent, with computers, mobile phones and remote controls for your gadgets.

Geminis are much happier in stylish city living than in a log cabin in the back of beyond. You like space, but you prefer it in the inside of your home, not in your back garden. You also hate untidiness, and although you like plenty of space, you don't want it filled with clutter. Geminis also like most things in pairs, or furniture with a geometric shape, such as a square or oblong.

Due to their great love of languages, they are likely to have a study or library that is used quite a lot. It could even be out of bounds to the rest of the household because it is 'their' space.

 Working from Home

You love your home and it would suit you to have a business that is conducted either within or attached to your residence. It would be like a home away from home, which reflects what a Gemini is all about.

KARMA, LUCK AND
❉ MEDITATION ❉

In your past life, Gemini, you were highly progressive and intellectu-ally very demanding. In this present life, you have adopted many of these traits to make you the forceful, dynamic and powerfully persuasive individual you are today.

The lessons of your past life will have taught you that intellectual arrogance and snobbery are tolerated by few. Unfortunately, some of you will not have grasped this facet of your spiritual development.

You have an intellectual and eclectic view of life, Gemini. You also possess an incredible ability to communicate, and most of your good fortune in life will come through this amazing skill.

The quality of air predominates in the Gemini temperament. Your mental and emotional equilibrium are related to your pattern of breathing, which needs regulating to lessen your anxiety and bring you calmness and tranquility.

Other methods of balancing yourself spiritually and emotionally include the use of gems and metals. The green emerald, silver or gold are useful metals and stones to tap the energies of Mercury and the Sun. Venus is your beneficial planet, which means that love and creativity, as well as some forms of speculation, will be lucky for you.

You have a restless mind, Gemini. The day of Saturn is Saturday, and it would be beneficial for you to meditate on that day. This will help accelerate your spiritual evolution and powerfully appease the negative karmas associated with your planets. The essential oils of sandalwood, Himalayan cedar wood, pine and ylang ylang will soothe your busy nature and bring emotional balance.

On a karmic and spiritual level, Aquarius has a strong influence on those born under Gemini. Developing your higher mind, controlling and directing your thought processes, and not allowing trivial issues to impact on you are all part of the natural, spiritual movement towards self-development and personal evolution.

Your key phrase is 'I think', but this does not mean 'overthink'. Focus on what you're doing and don't let your mind become the master. Rather, it should be the slave. Learning to balance thought with emotion is your challenge.

Lucky Days
Your luckiest days are Wednesday, Friday and Saturday.

Lucky Numbers
Lucky numbers for Gemini include the following. You may wish to experiment with these in lotteries and other games of chance:

5, 14, 23, 32, 41, 50

6, 15, 24, 33, 42, 51

8, 17, 26, 35, 44, 53

Destiny Years
The most significant years in your life are likely to be 5, 14, 23, 32, 41, 50, 68, 77 and 86.

HEALTH, WELLBEING AND DIET

Gemini, nobody could accuse you of living life in the slow lane, could they? You are constantly on the move, either physically or intellectually, and it is a good thing that the winged messenger of speed, grace and versatility is your ruling planet, Mercury.

Gemini is an air sign and dominates the airways, lungs, shoulders, arms and hands. You need to keep yourself warm and avoid illness, especially in the winter months, to prevent succumbing to asthma, bronchitis or other pulmonary problems.

Geminis are prone to taking on too many tasks at once and constantly rush from one project to another. Take care to avoid mishaps, accidents or unwanted stress by managing your time and eating smaller meals in an environment that is conducive to your wellbeing.

Keep Active

Sports such as tennis, swimming, walking or yoga, coupled with meditation, will help settle your mind and nerves.

Green vegetables are an excellent source of dietary nutrition for you, mainly because the colour green is predominantly ruled by Gemini. Although most foods agree with you, make sure you don't overeat because you are too busy talking.

Lean, high-protein foods are excellent for nourishing your body and sustaining you throughout the day. Oats and other raw grains, such as muesli, eaten first thing in the morning, are ideal for the Gemini character.

✴ FINANCE FINESSE ✴

Gemini, you are confident that money will come from somewhere. It may be hard to explain to others, but you know it is true because this is what happens in your life, and probably always will.

As far as you are concerned, money is a necessary evil. When it comes to earning money, you enjoy juggling many tasks and are suited to being a salesperson. With your wonderful communication skills, you could probably sell ice to Eskimos! A freelance sales job would be ideal, as it gives you the flexibility that you desire in your working day. Your charisma will probably close the deal. Or the client might sign on the dotted line to get rid of you. Either way, the money will go into the bank.

Changeable and unpredictable, you enjoy spending money and rarely worry where the next dollar is coming from. After all, the dollars keep rolling in. You can't be bothered with balancing accounts as there are far more exciting things to do with your time. If your business partner is willing to manage the purse strings, so much the better!

GEMINI

AT WORK

A HUMAN BEING SHOULD BEWARE
HOW HE LAUGHS, FOR THEN HE
SHOWS ALL HIS FAULTS.

Ralph Waldo Emerson

GEMINI CAREER

IDEAL PROFESSIONS FOR GEMINI

Teacher

Mediator

Sales consultant

Inventor

Writer

Journalist

Tour guide

Travel agent

Variety is the spice of life for you, Gemini. Your mind is constantly on the move, and your career may reflect this as well. You are certainly not looking for a gold watch at the end of 50 years of service as our grandfathers did.

It would not be unusual for you to have several jobs in a short space of time when you first start out. You could have a nine-to-five job to pay the bills, as well as a job at night or on weekends that appeals to your particular nature. You are not afraid to try different things, but when offered a position that interests you, do your research before accepting the role.

With your mental agility and constant search for intellectual stimulation, you need to use your mind and rational powers to achieve a sense of satisfaction in your work. Accounting, bookkeeping, information technology, sales, public relations, advertising, secretarial work, publishing and journalism are ideal for you.

As a creative creature, you need space to explore this side of your nature. You are not suited to being stuck in a dusty cubicle away from light and unable to communicate with your work colleagues. This would be a living death for you, and it would make you extremely unhappy.

Although you are not scared to try new things, you have a tendency to be overconfident in areas where you have little experience. If this happens, ask someone who is wiser or has more experience so that you can add to your considerable knowledge.

If it is a managerial position you are considering, your employers will know that you have the physical and mental energy to take on almost anything. With your capabilities, Gemini, you'll have a successful and fulfilling professional life.

✻ GEMINI BOSS ✻

If you are working for a Gemini boss, don't worry too much about the procedures manual as it will be shredded paper tomorrow.

Gemini bosses are brilliant thinkers who always come up with fresh ideas. They also need employees who will 'go with the flow'. As Gemini is a twin sign, it can be difficult to decipher what your Gemini boss is talking about as he or she may give you two different ideas about the same thing.

Gemini bosses sometimes think on more than one level at a time, and if you cannot immediately grasp a concept, you will get left behind. They will move on to the next project while you are trying to figure out the result of the previous one.

QUICK RESOLUTIONS

If a disagreement or problem arises, the Gemini boss will appreciate it if you go to them for a speedy resolution. They like to use their reasoning powers to reach a mutually satisfying decision.

Gemini bosses will listen to their employees as they are keen to keep things moving along, but you must never try to outsmart them. Their ego can't cope with it, and you will lose in the long run. You can help them, however, by containing their energy. Geminis can spread themselves too thinly.

A Gemini boss loves to talk, travel and be surrounded by subordinates and co-workers. They are a very social sign, and lunch with clients will probably be in a restaurant—and not necessarily a local one. They have large networks due to their excellent communication skills, and they like to keep in touch and know everything that is happening in the business.

✦ GEMINI EMPLOYEE ✦

If you are casting your eye around to find the Gemini employee in your office or workplace, just look for the person who is multi-tasking. This is usually a good indication that there is a Gemini on the payroll.

The Gemini employee has a spring in their step and a sparkle in their eye as they go about their daily duties. If they are not happy, they won't be working there. Geminis don't stay where their creativity and communication skills are not being utilised.

Gemini individuals always seem to have something to say, and there is generally a lot of wisdom or experience behind their opinions. They make excellent sales people, and with their love of words they are likely to come up with the latest company slogan. Give them the tools to express themselves and they will reward you tenfold.

Geminis can gossip and be a bit mean-spirited if they get bored, so the idea is to keep them busy and out of trouble. They talk and move fast, which is why their workspace needs to be clear enough for them to come and go without slowing the pace. They don't have very good brakes!

There is nothing that a Gemini employee loves more than a brain-storming session. With their enthusiasm and creativity, this is right up their alley. They may crack jokes and make small talk along the way, but they will get things done.

Gemini employees love a fast-paced environment where things are happening all the time. They can, however, get a bit distracted by the details—which they see as boring—and the social activities that may be part of the job. Geminis also need time to develop their skills and strategies, which will give them the springboard to come up with new ideas.

If you have a Gemini employee, do yourself a favour and put that wonderfully engaging person on the front line and let them blossom. They are great front desk people, and they can engage readily with whoever comes through the door.

PROFESSIONAL RELATIONSHIPS: ✷ BEST AND WORST ✷

BEST PAIRING:
GEMINI AND ARIES

An air and fire element combination will certainly make sparks fly! The natures of Gemini and Aries are very compatible, and if you are considering a business partnership, it would be hard to find a better combination.

Geminis are intellectually curious and love sharing ideas, which sits very well with Aries. When you blow hot with the fire sign Aries, you could have quite a firestorm on your hands. Your partnership is ideally suited to developing a good business and making it profitable in the long term. Aries falls in the eleventh zone to your Sun sign, Gemini, indicating profitability, friendship and the fulfilment of lifelong desires.

Not only could this be a successful business partnership, but it is highly likely that you will also be good friends. You feed off each other with your intellectual and physical drive, and there is an ample amount of supportive communication and inspiration. These traits can be the cornerstone of a fledgling business that can grow into an empire—if you so desire.

Perfectly in Sync

Aries may seem impatient or irritable at times, but you are more than
capable of bringing them down to earth. They will also like the speed with
which you think and act, and for the most part you will be perfectly in sync.

You are a great communicator, Gemini, and Aries will appreciate
this quality in you. You can provide a solid background and Aries
can be the driving force for ideas to take flight and come to fruition.
You can also give Aries direction, but make sure that your egos
don't get out of hand. This is a danger for both of you, given your
particular personalities.

Gemini, you are probably intellectually speedier than Aries, but not
by much. Try not to outdo each other as the professional side of
your partnership could suffer. You work so well together that there
is no need for one-upmanship here. You each have your own skill
set, and once a common goal has been decided on, you can go
full steam ahead.

WORST PAIRING:
GEMINI AND SCORPIO

Scorpio may fascinate you when you first meet, but beware. They
may come across as the strong silent type, but for the most part

they are secretive and uncommunicative unless they have good reason for showing their hand.

Gemini, however, seems to have the uncanny ability of being able to get Scorpio to open up and communicate a little better. Scorpios are sensitive, extremely faithful and can be rather blunt, but they are controlling in every way.

A business partnership between the two of you would be prone to failure if you approach it with your usual casual attitude. Geminis can work with anyone on an equal footing, but the problem you will encounter with Scorpio is their driving ambition and instinctive need to dominate.

This could make you feel uncomfortable and stifle your creativity. As a commercial arrangement, there will be a battle of wills for power, and it is unlikely that Scorpio will back down. It is not in their nature, and you will get tired of always being the one to give in, even when you think you are right.

Your Scorpio partner will be brutally honest, while you are more diplomatic and use your communication skills to get your meaning across without hurting anyone's feelings. Because Scorpio is not always trustworthy, they will probe every idea you have before they agree to discuss it. This will eventually drive you nuts!

In a business partnership, there needs to be an exchange of ideas and plans to make the venture a success. You will have all your cards on the table, Gemini, while Scorpio will have theirs folded against their chest where nobody can see them. This imbalance of trust will make you feel that they are being sneaky about information that is necessary for the functioning of the business.

Gemini, you need to convince Scorpio that there must be open communication, trust and compromise for the business to survive, but these three words may be completely foreign to your Scorpio partner.

GEMINI

IN LOVE

HE WHO LEARNS BUT DOES NOT THINK,
IS LOST! HE WHO THINKS BUT DOES NOT
LEARN IS IN GREAT DANGER.

Confucius

ROMANTIC
❋ COMPATIBILITY ❋

Are you compatible with your current partner, lover or friend? Astrology reveals a great deal about people and their relationships through their star signs. In this chapter, I'd like to show you how to better appreciate your strengths and challenges using Sun sign compatibility.

The Sun reflects your drive, willpower and personality. The essential qualities of two star signs blend like two pure colours producing an entirely new colour. Relationships, similarly, produce their own emotional colours when two people interact. The following is a general guide to your romantic prospects with others and how, by knowing the astrological 'colour' of each other, the art of love can help you create a masterpiece.

The Star Sign Compatibility for Love and Friendship table rates your chance as a percentage of general compatibility, while the Horoscope Compatibility table summarises the reasons why. Each star sign combination is followed by the elements of those star signs and the result of their combining. For instance, Aries is a fire sign and Aquarius is an air sign and this combination produces a lot of 'hot air'. Air feeds fire and fire warms air. In fact, fire requires air. However, not all air and fire combinations work.

When reading the following, I ask you to remember that no two star signs are ever *totally* incompatible. With effort and compromise, even the most 'difficult' astrological matches can work. Don't close your mind to the full range of life's possibilities! Learning about each other and ourselves is the most important facet of astrology.

Good luck in your search for love, and may the stars shine upon you in 2014!

STAR SIGN COMPATIBILITY FOR LOVE AND FRIENDSHIP (PERCENTAGES)

	Aries	Taurus	Gemini	Cancer	Leo	Virgo	Libra	Scorpio	Sagittarius	Capricorn	Aquarius	Pisces
Aries	60	65	65	65	90	45	70	80	90	50	55	65
Taurus	60	70	70	80	70	90	75	85	50	95	80	85
Gemini	70	70	75	60	80	75	90	60	75	50	90	50
Cancer	65	80	60	75	70	75	60	95	55	45	70	90
Leo	90	70	80	70	85	75	65	75	95	45	70	75
Virgo	45	90	75	75	75	70	80	85	70	95	50	70
Libra	70	75	90	60	65	80	80	85	80	85	95	50
Scorpio	80	85	60	95	75	85	85	90	80	65	60	95
Sagittarius	90	50	75	55	95	70	80	85	85	55	60	75
Capricorn	50	95	50	45	45	95	85	65	55	85	70	85
Aquarius	55	80	90	70	70	50	95	60	60	70	80	55
Pisces	65	85	50	90	75	70	50	95	75	85	55	80

HOROSCOPE COMPATIBILITY
FOR GEMINI

Gemini with		Romance/Sexual
Aries		Gemini may talk too much, for Aries; there is plenty of fire and excitement
Taurus		Constant stimulation is needed for this relationship to work
Gemini		Talking about what you want and how you feel will fill in many hours
Cancer		Sensual, but difficulties with being rational
Leo		This could be the love affair you remember all of your life
Virgo		Virgo is too much of a prude for you

Friendship	Professional
✔ Intellectually, this could be a first class friendship	✔ A power struggle
✔ Keep finding ways to keep this friendship fresh	✔ Taurus may come across as intellectually superior
✔ An enjoyable friendship if you can keep your egos in check	✔ Great creativity and mutual understanding; they will always be on your wavelength
✘ Moody Cancer will drive you mad; you can't keep up with all the changes	✔ A good arrangement, but you will need time
✔ Leo will appreciate your talent and friendship	✘ Leo can be stubborn and a hard taskmaster
✘ You won't like Virgo's constant criticism	✔ Can be a great financial asset with their practical approach

Gemini with		Romance/Sexual
Libra		Libra really knows how to push your buttons
Scorpio		Great sexual chemistry and high energy levels
Sagittarius		Excellent match between the sheets; physically fulfilling
Capricorn		A sexual mismatch where Capricorn takes all
Aquarius		The sparks will fly with this match
Pisces		Pisces can make you happy, but only on some levels

	Friendship		Professional
✔	Intellectual, social and creative stimulation	✔	Long-term success can be yours
✘	Rollercoaster ride with this friendship	✘	You will need to stand your ground with Scorpio
✔	Your social life will be No. 1 on the agenda	✔	Sagittarius can be lucky for you
✘	This relationship will be like an obstacle course for you	✔	You can do well financially, but creativity will suffer
✔	Be prepared to put in 110%	✔	Aquarius can teach you a lot about business
✘	Confusion reigns supreme here	✔	Pisces can come up with some great ideas for your business

GEMINI
❖ PARTNERSHIPS ❖

Gemini + Aries

This can be a warm and exciting relationship as you both love sharing ideas. You have an incredible intellectual curiosity, and Aries will relate to this on so many different levels. Gemini likes to think things through, whereas Aries is more impulsive.

Gemini + Taurus

You have friendly planets in the zodiac, which is why you have a natural attraction to each other. Humour, socialising and sharing your relationship with close friends bring you both tremendous joys. On an intimate level, your fast pace may become your undoing with a Taurus partner. You need to exercise some patience.

Gemini + Gemini

Romance with the same star sign can be a bit hit and miss. After all, there are two sets of twins at play. Although communication is a strong point, there's every likelihood that overstimulation will turn this relationship into an aimless affair. One of you needs to give the relationship some meaningful direction.

Gemini + Cancer

In this pairing, Gemini is the brain and Cancer is the heart. This can be an excellent relationship if you both compensate for what may be lacking in the other. Gemini, you need to be more sensitive to what your partner is feeling, and Cancer needs to be more aware of what you are thinking.

Gemini + Leo

Air and fire is a good match astrologically. Like you, Leo is intelligent, social and dramatic by nature. You will need to be on your best behaviour and look your finest to walk arm in arm at any social engagement with Leo. Great friendship is the basis of your connection.

Gemini + Virgo

Mercury rules both of you, but that doesn't guarantee a successful relationship. You may have similar ideas, but how you bring them to fruition is very different. Virgo's precision may drive you mad after a while. You are a 'big picture' person and far more expansive than they are.

Gemini + Libra

Being air signs will give you social stimulation, intellectual satisfaction and a creative friendship. This could be the start of something special. You will inspire each other to try for bigger and better things. Your love of art and music will give you a sense of harmony in the relationship.

Gemini + Scorpio

Scorpio comes across as the strong silent type, but they are actually secretive and uncommunicative, except with Gemini. Geminis have the uncanny ability of getting a Scorpio to trust them, and under their cold exterior is a seething cauldron of passion. There is no compromise in a romance with Scorpio.

Gemini + Sagittarius

The fire of Sagittarius works well with the air of Gemini. Sagittarians are always looking for bigger and better things, and you could be part of that journey. You too, Gemini, have a mental curiosity, and you will intellectually stimulate each other. You can share great communication and have sexual compatibility as well.

Gemini + Capricorn

There is a bit of a speed difference here. Gemini is in full throttle and Capricorn can be in neutral gear. Capricorns are more concerned with issues of security, Gemini, and they may see you as a bit irresponsible. Not the best match of the zodiac.

Gemini + Aquarius

This relationship is compatible, but it is also extremely challenging. There are high energy levels, ideas and desires that need to be fulfilled, and this could place excessive demands on each of you. Aquarians can be stubborn and a little overwhelming at times, while you are more adaptable, but this relationship can work.

Gemini + Pisces

You like to think things through, but Pisces is off in some other place altogether. However, your spiritual connection with Pisces will allow you to feel sexually satisfied by them. This relationship can work because of your adaptability and the mystical connection between you.

PLATONIC RELATIONSHIPS: BEST AND WORST

BEST PAIRING:
GEMINI AND AQUARIUS

At some time in your life, you will come across an Aquarian. They can be quite 'out there' compared to you, Gemini, but somehow or other you can make a friendship work.

Aquarians are unsurprisingly rebellious; it is just in their nature. They are quite aware of this, but don't give it more than a nano-second's thought. They are freedom lovers and, as far as they are concerned, the world is theirs for the taking. They don't particularly follow any rulebook, other than the one in their own head.

Geminis are in awe of this attitude to life, and it reminds them that they, too, seek variety, excitement and intellectual development. Aquarians wring as much as they can out of life, and you are amazed by the freedom they acquire along the way.

You are both ruled by air and are intellectually suited. Your Aquarian friends can be quite stubborn at times, and they thumb their nose at convention. For the most part, you'll be able to relate to them, even if you do have a difference of opinion—and you will at some stage in your friendship—but you won't challenge them to the point of dispute, and your differences of opinion will be in a playful tone.

AN INTELLECTUAL MATCH

*With your mutual love of intellectual pursuits, you can often be
found at a political gathering, cultural event or spiritual festival.
You will never be stuck for something to do, as you have many
common interests that you can enjoy together.*

If you decide that you want to take the friendship a step further,
you can do this with absolute certainty that it will turn out all right.
Your combination of Gemini and Aquarius works just as well sexually as it does platonically.

WORST PAIRING:
GEMINI AND PISCES

Gemini and Pisces are not a good combination for a friendship.
You operate on totally different levels, and it would be very difficult
to establish common interests that would get this relationship off
the ground.

Although you, Gemini, can be moody and changeable, Pisces
takes this beyond anything you ever imagined. They have different
emotional wiring, and you won't have a clue what you are dealing
with. You will spend a lot of time and energy trying to work out
where they are coming from.

Geminis like to speak their minds, and are quite adept at communicating their thoughts. Pisces, on the other hand, are not always
as forthcoming, and you will feel that they are holding something
back.

While Gemini is intellectual and being verbal is part of your basic temperament, Pisces is more intuitive. You both change your mind about as often as the weather, but you are motivated by different things.

Pisceans are more spiritual, and they may find you are a little superficial, Gemini. If you can show them that you have depth, you may be able to change their minds. Unfortunately, you come across as too flighty for their taste.

Gemini and Pisces can have some great adventures together, but there will always be ups and downs, and rarely will you be on the same intellectual or emotional level. You are poles apart in so many ways.

SEXUAL RELATIONSHIPS: BEST AND WORST

BEST PAIRING: GEMINI AND LIBRA

Here we have two air signs that are elementally suited to each other. Your personalities will naturally mingle, appreciate and love each other, and you are stimulated socially, intellectually and creatively by your friendship. These are the building blocks for something special.

There will be a natural flow of communication between you, and you will feel free to express yourself in whatever way turns you on, so to speak. Libra is the fifth star sign from Gemini, which is regarded as creative, romantic and sexually positive. Your mind will be stimulated and your physical inclinations will be taken care of as well.

You are wonderful communicators and both enjoy the company of friends, which are strong points when it comes to establishing a partnership. There will be times, however, when you will have a difference of opinion, and there will be no backing off for either of you. Making up afterwards will be worth it.

Imagination and communication will be at the forefront in your dealings with each other. You both dislike the humdrum of daily life and will continually reach for bigger, better and brighter things. You will both take pleasure in watching each other develop and in growing together.

The air signs are culturally curious and artistically gifted. You both seek interests that engage the more refined aspects of yourself, such as art, music and even humanitarian work, which will give you a sense of connectedness to your fellow man. These pursuits will also bring harmony to the relationship.

It would be unwise to think that this pairing will always be joyous and peaceful. Librans naturally try to find a balance, but may not always be successful, no matter how much they want it. And you, Gemini, are not always in a state of equilibrium, are you?

Sexually, you stimulate each other tremendously, and you are also mutually affectionate. When you say you love each other, that is exactly what you mean. For the most part, you are well suited on many levels and there is a natural bonding between you. There is no limit to what you can achieve together!

WORST PAIRING:
GEMINI AND CAPRICORN

This is certainly not high on the list of best matches, but there are some positives along the way. Let's try and find some, shall we?

You have probably heard the expression 'less is more', and this is the case with Capricorn. There is a difference in quantity and quality between these two star signs. Gemini is fast, versatile and adaptable in their way of doing things, whereas Capricorn is measured, slower and less willful in their approach.

Capricorn can be far more conventional than you, Gemini, and they can make you feel stifled. They don't readily respond to your childlike attitude, and it won't propel them into a more carefree lifestyle. If you are trying to get them to be more progressive in their daily attitudes, you are basically wasting your time.

CAPRICORN TOO STITCHED UP

Gemini will often feel that their Capricorn partner is tight-fisted and that they worry about security far too much. It is difficult for Capricorn to approach each day with a casual attitude. They are more stitched up than you, Gemini, and don't have your carefree approach to life.

If you can gain their trust by supporting them in their ventures and need for security, they'll be willing to meet you halfway. However, this will be more to their benefit than yours, Gemini. This control may also spill over into your sexual relationship as Capricorn has a tendency to hold back in matters of physical intimacy. Capricorn partners need someone to help them unwind, but you may not want to spend much time on this aspect of your relationship.

Gemini and Capricorn have different approaches to sexual intimacy. You, Gemini are light-hearted as you are ruled by the youthful Mercury, and this allows you to bring a lot of playfulness into the relationship. But this doesn't mean that it will turn on the rather dour Capricorn. You'll need to give them time to warm to you and express the deeper passionate element of their nature, which is there but not always in evidence.

If you are determined to stay in this relationship, you may find that money, or the control and power it gives, will be a sticking point farther down the track. This means that you will need to separate power issues from the sexual side of your relationship if you want it to work.

QUIZ: HAVE YOU FOUND YOUR
❀ PERFECT MATCH? ❀

Do you dare take the following quiz to see how good a lover you are? Remember, although the truth sometimes hurts, it's the only way to develop your relationship skills.

We are all searching for our soul mate: that idyllic romantic partner who will fulfill our wildest dreams of love and emotional security. Unfortunately, finding true love isn't easy. Sometimes, even when you are in a relationship, you can't help but wonder whether or not your partner is right for you. How can you possibly know?

It's essential to question your relationships and work on ways to improve your communication and overall happiness. When meeting someone new, it's also a good idea to study their intentions and read between the lines. In the first instance, when your hormones are taking over, it's easy to get carried away and forget some of the basic principles of what makes a relationship endure.

You're probably wondering where to start. Are you in a relationship at the moment? Are you looking for love but finding it difficult to choose between two or more people? Are you simply not able to meet someone at all? Well, there are some basic questions you can ask yourself to discover how suited you and your partner are. And if you don't have a partner, consider your previous relationships to improve your chances next time.

The following quiz is a serious attempt to take an honest look at yourself and see whether or not your relationships are on track. Don't rush through this questionnaire. Think carefully about your practical day-to-day life and whether or not the relationship you are in genuinely fulfils your needs and the other person's needs. There's no point being in a relationship if you're gaining no satisfaction out of it.

Now, if you aren't completely satisfied with the results you get, don't give up! It's an opportunity for you to work on the relationship and improve things. But you mustn't let your ego get in the way as that's not going to get you anywhere.

As a Gemini, you're committed to intellectual understanding and communication. You need a partner who understands your need for connectedness at an ideas level. If you relate to your partner in this way, you have a better chance of success. You have certain unique requirements in order to be happy in your romantic life. So here's a checklist for you, Gemini, to see if he or she is the right one for you.

Scoring System:

Yes = 1 point

No = 0 points

- ❓ Is he/she original and versatile?

- ❓ Does he/she have a good sense of humour?

- ❓ Does he/she mentally captivate you, and keep you surprised and excited?

- ❓ Is he/she secure and open enough not to feel threatened by your ever-changing interests?

- ❓ Can he/she provide you with emotional stability?

- ❓ Is he/she passionate towards you?

- ❓ Does he/she give you enough attention?

- ❓ Is he/she proud to introduce you to the world, and show his or her love for you?

- ❓ Does he/she surprise you with thoughtful things, like a hidden note or a holiday for two on a beautiful island?

- ❓ Is he/she a good conversationalist?

- ❓ Is he/she open and communicative?

- ❓ Is he/she open to doing innovative things together?

- ❓ Does he/she make you feel excited every time you see him or her?

- ❓ Does he/she mentally and emotionally stimulate you?

Have you jotted down your answers honestly? If you're finding it hard to come up with the right answers, let your intuition help you, and try not to force the answer. Of course there's no point in turning a blind eye to treatment that is less than acceptable, otherwise you're not going to have a realistic appraisal of your prospects with your current love interest. Here are the possible points you can score:

8 to 16

A good match. This shows that you and your partner enjoy a healthy understanding and reciprocate just the way you need. However, this is no reason to be slack out of complacency. You must continue working and improving your bond to make it shine more brilliantly than it does now.

5 to 7

Half-hearted prospect. You need to work hard at building your relationship and engage in honest self-examination. It takes two to tango, so you're obviously aware that you are both to blame. Go through each question systematically, making notes of areas where you can improve yourself. Undertaking this self-examination will guarantee favourable shifts in your relationship. But if things don't improve in spite of the effort, it may be time for you to rethink your future with this person.

0 to 4

On the rocks. I'm sorry to say that this relationship is completely devoid of basic mutual respect and understanding. It's likely that the two of you argue a lot. Your partner is also completely oblivious to your emotional needs. This is the perfect example of incompatibility. The big question is: Why are you still with this person? This requires some brutally honest self-examination on your part. You need to see whether there is some inherent insecurity within you that is causing you to hold onto something that has outgrown its use in your life. You may also be a victim of fear, which is preventing you from letting go of a relationship that no longer fulfils your needs. Self-honesty is the key here. You need to make some rather bold sacrifices to attract the right partner into your life.

2014
YEARLY OVERVIEW

ONLY THOSE WHO DARE TO FAIL GREATLY
CAN EVER ACHIEVE GREATLY.

Robert F. Kennedy

❈ KEY EXPERIENCES ❈

You idealism is at an all-time high throughout 2014, and as Neptune edges its way through the upper part of your horoscope, you'll find yourself dreaming about your life and the goals that you can achieve.

But dreams require a practical plan, money and other resources, which may not be available immediately. Saturn in your zone of work and service indicates that you have to focus clearly on the small stuff before you can achieve bigger dreams. Along with the Sun and the Moon, Venus, Mercury and Pluto occupy the important shared resources zone of your horoscope in the first week or two of the year, and this sets the trend for how you will deal with this aspect of your life.

With Mars impacting on your personal relationships, creativity and love affairs, there is no doubt you will be excited about these prospects. And with Uranus also occupying your zone of friendships, this should be a year when you will endeavour to do things a little differently. Associate with those who are unusual and spontaneous, and create a more exciting path in the area of romance and friendships throughout the coming 12 months.

ROMANCE AND
❦ FRIENDSHIP ❦

Anything traditional or conservative will leave you cold this year, Gemini. You are after something quirky, progressive and out of the ordinary. You won't settle for a dull routine when it comes to love in 2014. Those who are in a relationship with you are on notice! They need to step up to the plate and be ready for an adventure called love.

With Mars and Uranus dominating this area of your relationships, you are likely to undergo disputes or at least differences of opinion. As mentioned earlier, Neptune in the upper part of your horoscope is the most elevated planet as 2014 commences, and you will find yourself fantasising about the things you want. If these fantasies don't become reality, you could be in for some challenges.

Those of you already involved in relationships may feel that your spouse or partner is too demanding. Making compromises may be difficult, as you are strongly motivated by a sense of freedom and independence, even though you are tethered to the obligations of your relationship. Find a way to inject the sparkle and passion that we all want in our relationships. Not only will it keep your love affair going, but it will make it all the more exciting.

It is a year of sudden changes, perhaps even abrupt upheavals, in your social affairs. This is usually the case when Uranus is in the area relating to friendship. Uranus has been in this area for a little while, but many of you will now start to feel its impact on your life. This planet will bring changes, but they won't be slow and expected. They will be significant changes that happen without warning.

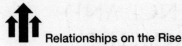

Relationships on the Rise

It is vital to know when some of these important changes will take place for you, Gemini, and it looks like Venus and Jupiter are key planets in this area of your life.

Interestingly, Jupiter is retrograde, in reverse motion, in the first part of the year, and this continues until the 6th of March. You could expect the difficulties and reappraisals you are going through to be resolved by this time. Around the 21st of the same month, the Sun moves to the zone of social activities, stimulating you to expand your social circle and meet with some unusual people, which I mentioned in the first part of your forecast.

March will be a significantly uplifting time as Venus enters into a powerful relationship with Mars, which happens to be in your zone of love affairs. Expect some fairly passionate experiences after the 30th of March.

That idealism I spoke about also reaches fever pitch after the 12th of April when Venus and Neptune join in the highest part of your horoscope. Many of you will realise what you want in your relationships and dreams, and expectations of love will become clear in your mind. The operative words here are 'in your mind'. This is because what you dream is not necessarily what will come to pass. You need to strategise ways of making your dreams a reality.

Your zone of friendship is once again lifted into a beautiful space after the 3rd of May when Venus makes contact and urges you to express your love and receive it from your peers and new friends. But be careful not to demand too much from others because Pluto may make you a little obsessive and unrealistic in your expectations.

You may do some unusual things after the 9th of July when the Sun and Uranus trigger those rather progressive attitudes I talked about earlier. After the 24th of July, love and work significantly overlap, but be careful, because you don't want to muddy the waters of your work activities with romantic interplay.

Some of the other significant dates that give you wonderful opportunities in love include the Mars and Neptune aspect on the 7th of August, and the Venus and Uranus aspect on the 25th. Be careful after the 14th of September when Mars enters your zone of marriage. Arguments and differences of opinion can mar what is usually a good connection between you and someone else.

The 9th, 14th and 28th of October, along with the 5th, 21st and 27th of December, are all important dates that punctuate the year with interesting and unusual developments in the love life of many Geminis.

❋ WORK AND MONEY ❋

Harness Your Moneymaking Powers

Making money can be summed up in an equation:

$$m \text{ (\$ money)} = e \text{ (energy)} \times t \text{ (time)} \times l \text{ (love)}$$

If one of these factors is not present—for example, energy or love—you could still make money, but you won't be ideally fulfilled in the process.

It's important to grasp the universal laws of attraction and success when dealing with money. It is also necessary to understand that when you love what you do, you infuse your work with the quality of attention, love and perfection. With these qualities you endow your work with a sort of electromagnetic appeal, a power that draws people to your work and makes them appreciate what you do. This generates a desire for people to use your service, buy your products and respect you for the great work you do. This will elevate you to higher and higher positions because you will be regarded as someone who exercises great diligence and skill in your actions.

Gemini, what powers within you are going to help you observe how others make money and put that knowledge into practice? One of the key ideas I want to share with you is Other People's Money (OPM). By understanding how to use seed funding, you can make more money and set in motion the wheels of success, even with little capital. Using other people's money rather than your own is a tried and tested method of growing your business. Venture capitalists and bank managers will listen to your ideas, but you must overcome your fear first.

This year, the recurring theme is idealism, dreams and ambitions, as shown by Neptune. Jupiter is an expansive planet, but it sometimes causes you to overdo things, and we can see that it is in an excellent place within your zone of income up until July, after which it moves to the arena of communication and contracts. The first part of the year may involve careful thinking, planning, observation and investigation, as well as discussions with experts to clearly map out what you want to do. I can't stress this aspect of your financial success enough. The Gemini mind is often as fickle as the wind, jumping from one subject to another. You need to slow things down and pick a particular topic or business plan and stick to it. This is important if you are to find your niche and make your talents work for you.

Work may be difficult this year, but because I see an excellent aspect—a trine between lucky Jupiter and focused Saturn—the financial remuneration you are looking for is likely to occur, but only if you keep your head down and your bottom up! When Jupiter transits to the third house of communication, you'll be able to solidify the plan, sign contracts and move speedily towards your ambition.

There are some other tips that I need to share with you, and these are of the utmost importance. Because the sudden and unpredictable Uranus is in the area for profitability, you must be prepared for change. This can happen suddenly, and if you are not used to saving for a rainy day, it may throw you off balance.

My strong recommendation is for you to save at least 10 or 15 per cent of whatever you earn, irrespective of how stable and secure you feel. That way, when the fluctuations of life occur, you will not feel buffeted about like a small paper boat in high seas.

Take a leaf out of other people's books after September and you will become more connected with others in business. You can do this through education, observation and day-to-day experience, but you need to put your ear to the ground and keep your eyes open and learn the lessons of those who have trod the path before you. This way you will avoid blunders that can distract or obstruct you from achieving your goals.

 Tips for Financial Success

Mars is the dominant force in your finances throughout 2014, so looking at its transits will give you a clearer picture of what's happening in that area of your life.

Excessive waste must be avoided around the 9th of January, as well as frivolous speculation around the 17th when Venus and Jupiter challenge expansive Mars. Hold onto your money, and don't think that you can get something for nothing.

Profitability is high after the 21st of March. You may not expect a bonus or cash surplus to arrive at this time, but when it comes, do not blow it all at the club on a Friday night. Put money aside whenever you feel that you've got an additional amount on hand.

Be wary of expenses after the 20th of April when the Sun moves to the twelfth zone of your horoscope. At this time, Jupiter will also challenge Uranus, and those profits I mentioned earlier may dry up rather quickly when outgoings exceed your income.

SOCIAL OPPORTUNITIES

As Venus enters your zone of profitability, friends may be instrumental in helping you earn more after the 3rd of May. There could be social engagements you don't want to miss as these can be perfect opportunities to extend your network of business and financial connections.

You will have to work harder after the 26th of July, when Mars enters your zone of workplace activities. Disputes with co-workers and getting distracted by mundane and trivial things must be avoided. Keep the compass pointing north, and remember that the small things you get involved in can get out of hand and undermine your efforts at earning more money.

The 5th, 9th and 14th of October are all good dates when you can expect extra cash and a small win if you are predisposed to a little gambling. But don't go overboard!

Challenges with tax and business partnerships after the 26th of October require a level head and practical solutions. The end of the year finishes on an excellent note, especially leading up to the 27th of December, just after Christmas, when Mars and the Sun provide you with additional energy to go out and earn more money.

Career Moves and Promotions

The tenth house of your horoscope is the key area for work, achievements and promotions. As mentioned earlier, Neptune is in this area at the start of the year, and whilst this is a planet of idealism, it can also wreak havoc and confusion if you are not careful to discriminate between the job offers and promotional opportunities that are being presented.

February is usually a great time for Gemini to make their move, particularly between the 19th and 25th. Around the 24th, make sure your rose-coloured glasses aren't making you see more than is there.

The period between the 6th and 20th of April is another favourable time when your powers of persuasion, good looks and general air of confidence will make a positive impression on those who are going to hire you or give you a chance to prove yourself in a more responsible position.

From the 25th of April up until the 29th, Venus and Saturn have a very steadying influence on your work, and the eclipse of the 29th means that some hidden talents may come to the fore and give you the edge against your competitors.

Venus and Neptune are in favourable aspect on the 24th of July and again on the 28th of October, which is an excellent omen for your work. You can make an impact again when Venus enters the seventh zone of your horoscope on the 17th of November. An opportunity on the 5th of December is fortuitous, but don't procrastinate, as Saturn's entry into the same sector on the 24th of December, the day before Christmas, may slow things down for you.

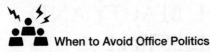 **When to Avoid Office Politics**

You need to use your excellent ability to multitask throughout the coming 12 months. You could be so distracted by work, money and other personal affairs that you may take your eye off the ball and not realise that people are conspiring to undermine you.

If you are too friendly with these people, then you are committing a big blunder this year. Keep your distance, be cordial, and don't divulge too much information to those who might otherwise harm your professional prospects.

The Sun and Saturn are not favourable on the 12th of February, but on the 14th of March, any rift between you and other co-workers can be healed. Again, don't ingratiate yourself, and maintain a fair degree of distance. The 30th of March may also create some cool responses between you and others you work with.

When the Sun enters the secretive zone of your horoscope between the 20th and the 29th of April, take care to watch your back. An ally may assist you after the 3rd of May.

The enemy of your enemy is a friend, so you must be mindful of that after the 26th of July when you can get someone else to do your dirty work. The Sun and Venus enter the sixth zone of enemies on the 23rd and 24th of October, which means that misunderstandings or arguments over money can escalate out of control. Make sure you have everything in writing, and clarify loans and other financial matters to everyone's satisfaction.

HEALTH, BEAUTY AND
❧ LIFESTYLE ❧

 Venus Calendar for Beauty

Venus, the planet of love, is friendly to those born under Gemini. This year, Venus will commence its transit in your eighth house of sexuality and deep emotional transformations. This is a time when you should allow your inner beauty to speak so that others can tap into the real you!

You are fortunate when Venus enters the luck, travel and education portion of your horoscope on the 6th of March. There will be some interest in acquiring foreign art objects, or even fashion accessories, that can highlight your rather unusual temperament. You are also attractive to others through your magnetic appeal around the 30th of March.

Your working life is augmented by your beauty and suave manner on the 6th of April when Venus enters your zone of career. You will be very alluring, but be careful not to abuse this power around the 12th of April when Venus conjoins with Neptune.

Others will definitely notice you throughout May and June, when Venus enters your zone of friendship. This is also a part of the zodiac that fulfils one's life-long desires. The way you present yourself and the beauty quotient you exude will definitely have an impact on your overall success in life.

Beauty can sometimes be tasteless, as exhibited by the Venus and Mars square on the 28th of August. Even though you are beautiful, you may not necessarily attract beautiful people. Keep your standards and integrity at the highest possible level.

Family, relatives and others you are close to will have some good advice for you, and although you may not like what they have to say, their suggestions for improving your looks and fashion should be taken to heart.

On the 5th, 11th and 21st of December, use your loving Venus energies to make a bold statement to the world around you. This is definitely a year when beauty can assist you in fulfilling your dreams.

Showing off Your Gemini Traits

When I tell you that you need to make the most of your characteristic zodiac traits, you may think that you need to do more, Gemini, but this isn't true. You won't have to try too hard to make an impact this year. Don't talk with your clever tongue! Let your facial gestures, the pauses between your sentences and the twinkle in your eye communicate for you.

Yes, you are the master communicator, but this year I am asking you to investigate non-verbal communication, gestural impact and other modalities for bringing out the best in your Gemini personality. By doing this, you'll discover a whole new vista of power, influence and success. Did you know that most of our communication is non-verbal? Think about that before you speak.

As an exercise, try turning down the volume on your TV set and observe what's going on when the actors interact. You will be surprised to see just how much is communicated when you can't hear what they're saying. This is one of the best pieces of advice I can give you for bringing out your best Gemini traits.

 Best Ways to Celebrate

You want lots of fun this year, but celebration needs to be done in a way that is not going to overextend your physical and mental energies. With Mars in your fifth house until July, you will have a tendency to spend too much time with people. This is understandable because we are trained from a young age to socialise, and we believe that having fun, nightclubbing and being with a lot of people is a natural way to enjoy ourselves.

That you have a cluster of planets within the transformative zone of your horoscope in January tells me that your spirit is seeking different sorts of enjoyment. The next chapter will explain why, but try to expand your view of enjoyment so that it is less material or social this year.

Because Neptune continues to play out for many years in your highest horoscope zone, your enjoyment will be through creative activities within your work. Remember, I'm using the words 'enjoyment' and 'celebration' interchangeably this year. Ordinarily, celebrations are occasions such as birthdays and anniversaries when we enjoy ourselves a little bit more than usual; but this year you need to take the concept of celebration further and incorporate it into everything you do, particularly your work. It's through enjoying the moment and focusing creatively and lovingly on every aspect of our lives that living becomes a celebration.

KARMA, SPIRITUALITY
AND EMOTIONAL
✳ BALANCE ✳

The first person you must be good to is yourself, Gemini. Stop putting others first. If you can't love yourself and give yourself the best, there is no way you can help anyone else. This year, the spiritual advice for you is to break free of people who are holding you back or forcing you to perform under par. By the same token, the electric and unpredictable energies of Uranus and Mars caution you not to go to extremes. You need to channel your electrical spiritual energy into clear, inner understanding.

The planet Uranus, your principle planet of past karma, receives several important aspects, and one of those tells us that you may go overboard on the 26th of February when Jupiter challenges Uranus. Waste, excessive expenditures and faulty judgement—all based on the desire to understand and grow—may push you onto the wrong path, so be careful. You do, however, have some excellent karma coming to fruition around the 3rd of May when Venus enters the eleventh house of fulfilment.

Connecting with like-minded, spiritually aware and evolved individuals is the quickest way to accelerate your own evolution. After September, you may find your friendships changing because you'll desire more nourishment for the soul.

The Sun enters into the fifth zone of future karma on the 23rd of September. This zone of your horoscope also says a lot about your creative impulses. Developing a talent, hobby or love is the fastest way to spiritual liberation or inner freedom. Work hard to discover what this is, and by the 30th of September you'll be able to make some important spiritual and karmic breakthroughs.

On the 27th of November, your two important karmic planets, Venus and Uranus, enter into a lovely aspect that affects friends, spouses and lovers. Harmony will prevail, and if you can capture the essence of what's going on in your relationships and repeat this, you may find the right formula for spiritual success in 2014.

2014
MONTHLY & DAILY PREDICTIONS

THERE IS NO FUTURE FOR A PEOPLE
WHO DENY THEIR PAST.

Adam Clayton Powell, Jr

❈ JANUARY ❈

Monthly Overview

The first month of 2014 is an intense one, and much of your energy will be focused on emotional and possibly even sexual issues. The New Moon on the 2nd brings with it a vital energy that can help you break through some of your inner complexes and fears. Money should work well for you when Jupiter transits your zone of finance.

1   There is no need to argue your point today because it will only inflame the situation. Don't let Mercury and Mars get the better of you. Be soft, slow and easy in the way you get your point across.

2   You can cleverly work your way out of a financial problem, but you need to stay focused on the key issues. Distractions should be eliminated.

3   Travel is on the cards today, and you have a great need to get away from your normal humdrum life. Take a mini adventure to relax yourself.

4 Your creativity is excellent right now, and the Moon and Mars are giving you spontaneous insights and a love of new hobbies. Explore these.

5 Work is high on your agenda, but you may not know where to start. There is no shame in asking others to help you on this matter.

6 It is a lucky day today, but if you are looking in the wrong direction, you'll miss the opportunities that prevail. Remain receptive and don't dismiss what you might consider trivial incidents.

7 Friendship, social alliances and group activities dominate your activities. A sudden meeting could be fortuitous.

8 You are angry and need to let off steam. Connecting with a trusted friend can help you clear the air.

9 Your sentimentality is eroding time and valuable emotional energy. Don't let daydreaming spoil your day.

10 It's a low-key sort of day and you need your space. Don't let others disturb you.

11 You may incur a loss through your own extravagance and carelessness. Learn from your mistakes, but don't harp on about it.

12 You are emotional just now, but if you direct that energy into your nearest and dearest relationships, it can work in your favour.

13 You are energised just now and have abundant physical and mental strength. Sports and outdoor activities are favourable.

14 If you are emotional about money, you'll falter. Take your time when making decisions, particularly if you are the one who has to pay.

15 You're impulsive with people today, and you may assume that someone likes you more than they do. You are setting yourself up for a fall. Take care.

16 You are more deliberate and careful in the way you execute your work at the moment. Don't be afraid to take your time, even if others are rushing you.

17 It is time to review your contracts and other agreements. By being diligent and not sweeping problems under the rug, you'll increase your chances for success.

18 Someone may be cool and aloof just now, but chasing them and trying to resolve problems will only make you seem weaker. Wait until they are more amenable.

19 Domestic issues are high on your agenda. Talking to females within your family can give you a clearer perception of how to bring out more love in the family circle.

20 You have a spiritual insight today, but you may not know how to make it practical. Let the idea percolate for a while.

21 You want a new love affair, but your options and social circle of influence may be limited. This could relate more to imagination and fantasy.

22 Speculations will only cause loss. Don't gamble unless you have all the facts.

23 You may be wasteful with money again. If you have to purchase someone a gift, try not to overspend.

24 Health issues may bother you, but these are related to excessive work. Slow your pace.

25 Your mental acuity is sharp, and your tongue is fiery. You may need to attack someone, but they deserve it.

26 You are stepping away from the crowd to reappraise things. This is a great idea as you are too emotionally involved.

27   You want some progressive new friendships, so it is time to break free. Independence is your key word at present.

28   If you have a long-standing psychological issue, no matter how minor, now is the time to eliminate it.

29   A friend's unexpected behaviour may disappoint you. Don't dwell on this too much; you are magnifying the situation.

30   If you lose a game, don't take it too seriously. You need to be a good sport today.

31   The New Moon shows that you are ready to turn over a new leaf and implement your New Year's resolutions.

✴ FEBRUARY ✴

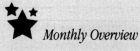

Monthly Overview

You want to travel, explore new horizons and meet new people, but your mind is divided, which is typical of your Gemini nature. At the same time, you're confused about certain work requirements. This needs to be addressed before you can feel comfortable about any sort of vacation. Unexpected expenses may complicate matters, especially after the 10th.

1   You have a brilliant idea for work or a new project, but you may feel scattered. Gather the threads and focus your attention.

2   Issues of love can be bound up in sexual matters. Express and resolve whatever issues have been bothering you.

3   Physical unwellness, minor health issues or previous injuries may start to improve. This means more energy for the things you love.

4 Being a step ahead of the crowd is not always good, particularly if you advertise it. Someone may have it out for you, so keep your ideas close to your chest.

5 Your dreams are vivid, and there may be some psychic experiences that will help you come to a conclusion over a problem. Trust your instincts.

6 You'll be in an investigative mood and may discover something that helps you financially. This could have been an oversight.

7 You need to spend more time than expected on a problem in your workplace. Don't cut corners as this will require more effort on your part.

8 You may come up with a solution at work that is great in theory but not in practice. Get feedback from others before implementing your plan.

9 Higher educational prospects will help you better yourself. Do you have the time, though? Perhaps an online or correspondence course is the way to go.

10 Children will bother you, and if you are a parent, you may need to have a few arguments to make your point. Money could be at the heart of the problem.

11 Your creative and spiritual instincts meet, but you may be ahead of your time with a concept. Break your idea into stages.

12 Your plan for implementing some work changes is obstructed by wilful people. Timing is everything.

13 You'll be injecting a lot of energy and time into something that will not be worth it. Rethink your priorities.

14 Don't mix friends with work and money. The temptation is there, but the results will be disastrous.

15 If you react too emotionally to professional circumstances that are out of your control, you may lose out financially and emotionally.

16 You could meet an old friend whose life changes have created such a dramatic rebirth that you want to follow in their footsteps. Now is the time to start.

17 Your emotions and willpower are out of sync at the moment. Try to develop harmony within if you want it to show on the outside.

18 You may be spending too much time on someone who is not reciprocating your feelings. Balance give and take if want an equitable partnership.

19 You are extremely attractive at the moment, and people around you, particularly those you work with, may drain your energies for their own purposes. Study other people's motives.

20 Your past and future karma converge today, and what you do, even though it may seem inconsequential, will have a significant impact on your future. Everything you do right now is important.

21 You have great feelings of affection and generosity, but you may give too much or pay an excessive amount for something. Compare prices.

22 You are charming today and can win the hearts of many! This is an excellent time to network and meet new people.

23 You are in the mood for love, but work matters may inhibit you from sharing time with your partner. A reschedule is necessary.

24 Your ideas are met with cautious optimism by superiors. Clarify matters by explaining or writing down what you have in mind.

25 Don't avoid taxation and other government or bureaucratic issues. They can make life easier for the moment, but problems in this area may snowball. Address these issues immediately.

26 You are too busy to keep your mind on the job and may lose something right now. Pay special attention to your wallet, keys and credit cards.

27 Don't allow your ego to obstruct someone's wise words of caution. Learn what you can from those who are more experienced.

28 A female in your family may be tight-lipped about a problem. This requires careful psychological strategising if you want to get to the bottom of the issue.

✤ MARCH ✤

Monthly Overview

Your work environment is due for a big change. Don't let the cloudy confusion of Neptune dampen your efforts to start something new, accept a promotion or seek work elsewhere. Unclear statements, messy fine print, and other promises need to be taken with a grain of salt. If uncertain about a course of action, wait!

1 You're tempted to sign on the dotted line or make an agreement with someone prematurely. Wait a couple of days until the dust settles.

2 You feel irate today and want things to happen more quickly. Your key word today is patience.

3 A friend may turn on you. Make sure you are not too trusting, particularly of those you work with.

4 Security is an issue just now, so make sure that you lock doors and install security alarms and other deterrents around your home and car.

5 If you focus too much on a problem, you'll cloud the issue. Try to get a different perspective by asking other people's opinions.

6 You feel confused or may not be able to express yourself adequately right now. Sometimes, non-verbal communication may be more effective. You need to study this.

7 You're treading water at the moment, and although you know what you want, the circumstances are obstructive. You need to go with the flow to reduce stress.

8 An employer or senior manager may throw a spanner in the works, which will make it difficult for you to complete your tasks. Have plan B ready.

9 You can communicate ideas through the written word. Any sort of advertising, news or global information will be of interest to you.

10 The transits are good today, and that long-awaited pay rise or bonus may finally arrive.

11 You are deliberate in your thinking, but you may lose an opportunity because you are too slow off the mark. Balance speed with circumspection.

12 It may be necessary to take up a new exercise regime. You've been slipping and may not realise just how much this is affecting your body, mind and emotions.

13 If you must travel or go out to lunch, it is time to try something different. Break out of your usual habits.

14 You feel victorious in some business strategy or planning. Those who previously didn't support you will change their minds.

15 You need to do some posturing today, particularly if you can't have it out fully with someone. Holding your ground will send them a distinct message.

16 You may catch someone out in some mischief, but you are confused about to how to deal with this. Don't react too quickly. Sit on it for a few days.

17 You're contemplating your future and want answers. Don't look outside yourself. The answers are often within.

18 Time is of the essence, and you may not be using it as constructively as you could. Pay careful attention to the 80/20 rule. You must get 80 per cent return on 20 per cent input, not vice versa.

19 The health of a child or a loved one may require a change of plans at this time. Don't be too concerned; this is a passing phase.

20 Your spiritual ideals may clash with your historic belief system. You need to look at the facts and explore the truth for yourself.

21 A friend may be in debt or experiencing some crisis. Your assistance should be limited to helping them help themselves.

22 You need to push for what is rightfully yours, especially in a professional context. If you are being too nice to others, you are never going to get your just deserts.

23 You can finally make some inroads in your career and impress others with your ideas. Taking the road less travelled will give you an advantage over others. You are unique today.

24 If you are sexually frustrated, you need to express your concerns to your partner. The one you love may be angry, but only because of their own frustrations.

25 You are dealing with some financial matters and need the help of experts. Don't try doing this alone.

26 Male figures could feature prominently in your life at present. Authoritative people, however, may cause you to lash out.

27 You may be youthful, exuberant and cheeky in the way you deal with others, particularly clients. This could win you some additional money, sales and, of course, friends.

28 You need to open up your environment to new energies. If you are feeling cramped and there is nothing in your life that is emotionally or spiritually stimulating, you must change this now.

29 Your nervous system may be strung out, but you need to chill out. Don't worry about what hasn't happened yet.

30 Your passions may lead to some indiscretion at this time. Try to think carefully about the consequences of your action, particularly if it is of an amorous nature.

31 You may be accused of saying or doing something, only to find that your defence makes you seem guilty. Silence is the answer.

☆ APRIL ☆

Monthly Overview

You'll be able to win the hearts of many during the coming month, and with Venus transiting the upper part of your horoscope, you'll be able to mix business with pleasure in a balanced way, opening up many new connections. Profits are strong and some unexpected earnings will surprise you. On the 6th, 12th and 16th there may be opportunities for increased cash flow.

---

1   You could feel like a prisoner today, but that's probably all in your mind. Freedom and constraint are states of being.

---

2   You may be called on to mete out justice today. Acting as a mediator between two parties is likely.

---

3   You will not have time to socialise, as documents and other tedious paperwork need to be looked at.

---

4   You are surrounded by books, and this means that you are overloaded with knowledge and responsibilities. You need to take a break to refresh yourself.

---

5 You are seeing the world through rose-coloured glasses. You could be in for a rude shock when reality hits home.

6 Sometimes the journey is so enjoyable that you lose your way. I am talking about life. Pleasure is only half the fun.

7 Your performance is based upon your strength at present. Make sure you are healthy and vital, otherwise you won't function properly.

8 Your living circumstances are cramped. You need to make space as there is too much clutter building up.

9 You may reminisce about the past, but don't play the comparison game. Every day is unique, and you should accept and be grateful for what you have.

10 You may feel as if you can fly right now, but this could be in your imagination. Make sure you have wings before you take to the skies.

11 If you are dealing with another woman's emotions, make sure that they don't overwhelm you. You need to be level-headed today.

12 It is hard to be yourself when you are dealing with someone who is straight-faced and unemotional. You may also feel that you are being scrutinised for no particular reason.

13 The world is as you see it today. Don't superimpose your moods on what's happening in your environment.

14 You may have outstanding legal matters that are bothering you. Address them now, even if it means paying some fines. This could relate to parking or speeding infringements.

15 Promising more than you can deliver is a recipe for disaster, especially if you do it with too many people. Payback time has arrived, and you may not have the time or resources to do it properly.

16 You need to have all your facts if you are going into battle just now. A professional rival may challenge you.

17 You're frivolous with money at a time when you can ill afford it. Count your pennies today.

18 You may wish to go back to your childhood or an earlier time when things were not so complicated. Once again, it is all a matter of attitude and what you're projecting.

19 You may miss someone who has gone away or is absent from your life. If you are still on good terms, make a call. Even if it is costly, tell them how you feel.

20 There is fire surrounding your finances. This can mean disputes or the energy to earn more.

21 The child in you is hiding, and you're scared to show your innocence for fear of becoming vulnerable. This is exactly what you need to do to experience a resurgence of life, love and laughter.

22 If you lecture others, you need to be careful that you are not judged by the same harsh standards. Don't get accused of asking others to do as you say and not as you do.

23 It is time for a bit of spring cleaning and minor repairs around the home. Don't overdo it as you may get carried away and spend more than you should.

24 You're the torchbearer today, and you may be asked to lead the way at work. This requires courage and confidence. Do you have what it takes?

25 Nature, peace and tranquillity are what you need just now. This can be environmental or something you project from within.

26 You are at a crossroads today. Which way will you go? Unfortunately, you have no clue and feel stuck. It's better to stay stuck than travel in the wrong direction.

27 You have to understand that money and wealth are based upon the laws of success. Simply put, whatever you believe will become your reality!

28 You are in a technical maze just now, Gemini. You need to use technology to move ahead, but may be afraid of the daunting task. Start gaining some more skills in this area.

29 You may involve yourself with someone, possibly a member of the opposite sex, who appears to be emotional. But you'll discover that this is masking some issues that you need to distance yourself from.

30 Prayer, meditation and inward reflection will be the way to deal with problems today. Don't use the rational mind.

✦ MAY ✦

Monthly Overview

You have a need to hide away, at least for the first couple of days of the month. Focus on your needs and don't be afraid to express this to the world around you. Heavy responsibilities occur up until the 10th due to the Sun and Saturn combination. Plan your work more carefully and be decisive with co-workers.

1 Remember that endings, such as the death of a relationship, are usually the beginning of something new. Look at what's happening as a transformation and major life lesson.

2 You have power, but you need to know how to use it. The letter 'i' is significant at the moment, and someone whose name begins with this letter may have a connection with you.

3 Your charisma is contagious at present, and friends will want to be with you. It's all systems go, but be careful not to become too much of a social butterfly.

4   Some financial deal may go sour because you haven't dotted your i's and crossed your t's. All is not lost, but you need to look at the problem fair and square.

5   Although you may have some success or breakthrough today, don't be too effusive in front of others. Envy may rear its ugly head.

6   If you are single and have a desire for someone, you need to exercise restraint. Balancing the masculine and feminine qualities in your nature is the key.

7   This is an excellent day for emotional satisfaction. Although your work and financial circumstances may bother you, you may experience some relief through a friend.

8   You can turn a failure into a success today. Look at the seeds of opportunity through something that has gone wrong.

9   Courage is your key word today, and even in the face of others who may pull you down, you can achieve a great deal in spite of them. Laugh it off.

10   Becoming a hermit for a day and reflecting upon your situation will yield gems of wisdom. Your totem today is the owl, symbol of knowledge and wisdom in the darkness of the night.

11 You may build something up to a magnificent level and then demolish it because you are not satisfied with it. As long as this is your doing, all will be well.

12 If you're feeling inadequate in a group or workplace situation, you must develop your intellectual confidence. If you want to be a leader, you need to stimulate the respect of others.

13 If you are working with people who have no passion for their work, you could run into obstructions. Someone born under Aquarius could be the cause of this problem.

14 There are endless possibilities today, but the choice is yours. You need to work through several scenarios to know which will suit you.

15 Discussing finances with your business partner or spouse will bring harmony. A compromise may be necessary.

16 If you take things for granted, you won't improve your situation, especially in love and relationships. Look more closely at people's personalities.

17 You will be worried about finances again, but worrying won't change things. You need to look at the cause of your lack and how you can attract more money through the laws of success.

18 Perfection, or doing your best work, is necessary if you want to improve your position in life. This also goes for your résumé. Try to work on it.

19 Whether you are a man or a woman, you have a nurturing instinct today. Use this to open your heart and help others.

20 You need to expand your horizons now. Don't limit yourself to your past self-image. Creatively visualise yourself in a better place.

21 Expressing your uniqueness may not be easy, as everyone is keeping you waiting. As Darwin said, 'Survival of the fittest requires adaptation'.

22 Some good fortune—emotional and material—may be yours. The letter 't' is significant.

23 Games of chance can pay off just now. Take a gamble on your career. It may be scary, but it will be fortuitous.

24 You have more talents than you give yourself credit for. A friend may point out a unique character trait or skill that you have overlooked.

25 Material gain is on the cards, and although this may not be sizeable, it will be enough to instil greater confidence and self-respect.

26 Those born under Taurus and Virgo can be helpful at present. Seek out their advice on financial matters.

27 Don't be a fool today by not listening to your body. If your inner voice is telling you is to stay in, take it easy and avoid others. Don't do the opposite.

28 The bonds of love are strong at present, and if you are in a relationship, this could be a day to kick-start your romance. Recollect the initial feelings you had for each other.

29 Relationships continue to bring joy and happiness. If you are in a relationship, you may choose to do something daring on your life path.

30 You have dominion over your environment, but you still consider yourself weak. Look at the power you have and use it wisely.

31 Someone may stab you in the back. Be mindful of other people's motives to stay a step ahead of them.

✤ JUNE ✤

Monthly Overview

Lucky financial undertakings give rise to optimism for your future success and security. Plan new work practices and business strategies, as Mercury, the Moon and Jupiter support you. Mars in the fifth zone makes you accident-prone, especially with Uranus in the opposite part of the heavens. Don't push yourself too hard in sport and competition.

---

1 You need to toe the line if you are in another person's environment. If someone has power, you need to observe how they function and use it in your own immediate circumstances.

---

2 You feel chained to your circumstances because you lack knowledge, or because your knowledge is not practical. That's easily remedied by looking farther afield and learning new things.

---

3 You may have had high expectations for someone, only to find that they are not what you expected. Study their history and background to find out who they are.

---

4   It's time to step up and take on a leadership role, at least temporarily. Others may look to you for guidance at this time.

5   If you are finding that members of your family are misbehaving, you have to understand that you are the example they look up to. Start with yourself.

6   You need to travel somewhere, but others may be demanding too much of your time. You need to prioritise today and not let others make you feel guilty.

7   If you've had cross words with someone, today is when you should make peace. Although the issues may be cloudy, make a start and build on it.

8   Tradition could bother you as you feel hamstrung by convention. You need to step outside the square for fun and profit.

9   If you are not successful in love, you at least feel that something is around the corner. One word of caution: never appear desperate or obsessive. Relax a little and love will come to you.

10   The power of the earth is essential for you right now. Better diet, more oxygen and getting your hands and feet dirty will anchor you and recharge your batteries.

11 The number 10 is lucky for you at present, as is a Virgo, who may assist you in earning money. Remember this.

12 A business partnership can commence now, but you each need to agree on a course of action that you are both equally passionate about.

13 You may feel grateful for the friendships that you have at present. This gratitude will be reciprocated, and your social affairs should run smoothly.

14 Going somewhere unexpected can be the best recipe for satisfaction and happiness. A sense of exploration should infuse your activities today.

15 You must blend hope with practicality to achieve success. You may reach some pinnacle in your career or meet someone who is famous or well known.

16 Don't make material gain and status the criteria for associating with people, particularly when it comes to love. Look at the heart, not the wallet.

17 You can improve your relationships with young people just now, and if you are a parent, all is well for a better future together.

18 You may be confronted by a harsh or even cruel character, and it may be someone you know. Try to avoid them.

19 You may lift someone's self-esteem today, particularly if they've helped you at some time in your life. This feeling of mutual appreciation represents the excellent energies of the Moon and Jupiter.

20 Hard work is necessary today, but your mind is not on the job. Sometimes it is better to take a break and return to the task with a fresh mind.

21 You could have an inspired moment when a problem is mysteriously resolved, much to your delight. Don't let this satisfaction turn into a big ego.

22 To win the approval or even financial support of others, you need to exhibit confidence. This is not in short supply today, so you should be successful.

23 You see yourself as the guardian of people or things, but remember that too much smothering may inhibit the development and growth of others.

24 Don't throw the baby out with the bath water today! Discriminate as to what needs to be eliminated and what can be retained. If you are too quick to make decisions, you may discard something of value.

25 If you know of someone suffering psychological or emotional problems, you could help them by taking them out and giving them a new perspective on life. Helping others will also help you.

26 Someone could disappoint you now, and it may be due to their lack of integrity. You have no control over people's actions, so don't take it to heart.

27 Interfering in other people's financial or family affairs is a no-no today. Don't comment on things that are none of your business.

28 A greater sense of harmony will prevail because you are able to share some words of wisdom with those who previously disagreed with you.

29 You've made a breakthrough and smell success on the horizon, but you may spend what you have before you actually earn it. Think of your credit card bills before being impulsive.

30 Problems in your relationships can now be put to bed. A better cycle is commencing.

✵ JULY ✵

Monthly Overview

Venus and Mercury make you lucky in love, but don't be too passionate as Mars continues its rounds in your fifth zone of love affairs. Mercury in retrogression causes you to make errors of judgment in love. You should ask the right questions if you want to get the right answers. Short journeys may occur in the first week of the month, and again after the 15th.

1   You are finding it hard to trust others, but burying your head in the sand is not going to unearth the truth. If you are afraid to confront reality, this will become an ongoing problem.

2   You have a love of family and need to feel that the love is reciprocated. You will make extra efforts to ensure that family unity prevails.

3   Harmony continues, but you may have a minor issue associated with money that will bother you.

4 You want more out of life, but how do you communicate that to others, especially if you feel as if you have been short-changed? Develop a better way of speaking to others.

5 Someone may be advocating a financial venture, but be careful, they may have a vested interest in the outcome.

6 You can always learn something from others, but you may feel apprehensive if the person doesn't seem as experienced. Don't discriminate against youngsters; they have knowledge as well.

7 There are some issues hanging in the balance, and your decision may impact adversely on someone else. You may need to be somewhat ruthless when it comes to drawing your conclusions today.

8 If you are being forgetful at present, you need to tattoo an idea in your mind to make sure you don't forget. Retaining facts and figures is essential today.

9 Someone may intrude in your life right now, particularly your relationships. You have to stand up and create the necessary space to prevent this from happening.

10 You could experience some gruelling work and demanding social pressures. Are you getting enough sleep?

11 If you are thinking of entering into a business partnership or alliance, remember that it is still a marriage of sorts. For some it can be bliss, and for others it can be a life sentence.

12 If you are losing things, you need to take an inventory of what's important and where it is. That way you'll know exactly where all of your valuables are at any given time.

13 Love, passion and people could be a bother, and even though you may like their attention, the social aspects may be too draining. Don't feel obligated.

14 If you are ambidextrous, you might have a good chance of pleasing everyone and finishing your work today, but you may not have enough time.

15 There is a chance that someone exotic may cross your path, but remember that proprietary, self-honour and respect should stand above all else.

16 You crave spontaneity, but you are in a stuffy environment and will be regarded poorly for acting out of the norm. Be selective and wait for different circumstances.

17 You will be enthralled by a short journey that will be educational during this phase. Philosophy, culture and the arts are appealing.

18 Remember that money is not the sole criterion for a good job. If you are looking for something new, bear in mind other benefits, such as the hours you will work. This can sometimes erode your pay packet and reveal the real value of the deal.

19 Don't react to derogatory remarks. You need to be prudent in the way you respond to an attack today.

20 Relationships should never degrade the people involved. If this is happening, you need to take time out and reappraise where you want to be.

21 By fostering cohesion in the family unit, you improve the outcome for all in the group. This is especially true for children and youngsters. Teach them the value of togetherness.

22 Someone may elude you, but don't be too suspicious. It may simply be a matter of timing.

23 You are sceptical about your profession, but try to think about those who are in dire circumstances. Today requires an attitude of gratitude.

24 Try to be more reliable, even if you are overloaded with work. Allocate more time for travel to give others a better impression of your commitment.

25 If you feel as though you are outnumbered, the old adage 'divide and conquer' may be apt today. Do battle on an individual rather than a group basis.

26 Taking stock of your workload is essential now. You may need to put this in writing and give it to someone in a superior position. If you don't ask for something, you won't get it.

27 You feel as if someone is trying to inspect your work. If this is the case, you mustn't crumble under the pressure. There may be something you can learn through this process.

28 You could be worried about security and the need to fortify your premises. It is always a good idea to be prepared for the worst.

29 Don't spend good money on something that's not worthwhile. This could relate to home renovations, where money could be better spent on new premises.

30 You must bring up the courage to do something you haven't done before. It may be frightening at first, but it will give you a great sense of power in the end.

31 You may feel uncomfortable when you are left out of a group activity. Analyse why you are being treated like an outsider.

☀ AUGUST ☀

Monthly Overview

You may be angry and will lash out at others who are either too slow or incapable of understanding your viewpoint. Mars and Saturn edge closer to an intense conjunction in your workplace, which could affect co-workers and their work ethics or attitudes. Flashpoints could be expected on the 10th, 11th, 12th, 16th and 18th.

1 Brevity is your key word at present. Don't ramble on if you have a point to make. Silence will make a much greater impact.

2 If everything is hunky dory, you don't need to create problems. Perhaps you've become addicted to this mindset. Just relax and enjoy the peace.

3 Someone may try to induce you to do something against your will. Your mind may feel accosted, but in your intellectually polished and charming manner, you can sidestep this problem.

4 Sometimes you need to pretend to be disinterested to stimulate someone's interest in you. You should try this tactic today.

5 With the Moon in your zone of love and marriage, and in favourable relationship to Venus, love is in the air. Make the most of this.

6 Why so glum, Gemini? The cup is not half empty, it is actually half full.

7 Categorise your receipts, expenses and other activities so that your mind won't be overwhelmed by chaos. You will be able to understand your finances much better this way.

8 Blindly following others is like the lemmings walking off the edge of a cliff in droves. You needn't follow the crowd today.

9 Whether you go to a five-star restaurant or small canteen in a back street, it's the company you keep that makes an event memorable.

10 If it is time to re-sign contracts, you need to look at a higher remuneration package. The hard aspects today indicate that you may be operating from a base of fear rather than self-esteem.

11 Working long hours may mean that you're leading a sedentary life at present. You need to motivate yourself to improve your health.

12 You feel buoyant and excited and anticipate good things today. This air of satisfaction breeds success.

13 You may be given a lot of information today. Distil the pertinent facts and discard the rest.

14 You are feeling a lot of love and affection for someone, but you may be suffocated in response. Take things slowly.

15 To divulge or not to divulge, that is the question. Passing on sensitive information may start a chain of gossip that will come back to haunt you.

16 You may experience some material difficulties because of someone you are associated with. You may be asked for a loan.

17 You could meet someone whose mannerisms are affected. Whilst this will irk you, you will have no choice but to put up with the situation to please another person.

18 If you need to be aggressive, do it with style. You have the gift of the gab, so use it diplomatically.

19 It is time to improve your position by surrounding yourself with allies. There is strength in numbers today.

20 You need to clean up your act, Gemini. You'll find that you are spending money on useless things and activities. You will be shocked at how much you could save by eliminating bad behaviours.

21 You need to motivate others to get the job done. This task may not be easy.

22 If someone is flattering you, you can rest assured that there is a hidden agenda. Read between the lines.

23 You mustn't be too sensitive if someone takes a swipe at your belief system. They've a right to believe what they want, even if they are a little hard on you. Setting a good example is the best way to counteract this problem.

24 There is no harm in haggling over a price if you think you can get a better deal. At the same time, it can be a lot of fun. Try it.

25 You don't need to confess your sins to a priest, but you may need to make an admission of guilt to someone to relieve your conscience.

26 It's frustrating when someone approaches you for advice and you know that they are not going to take it. You should meet this person with an attitude of indifference.

27 You need to remind someone just how valuable you are to them today, even if they are less than fair in their response.

28 You need to build a moat around yourself today, and don't forget the crocodiles. Keep friend and foe at bay to complete a task that you have postponed for too long.

29 You need to prepare for the coming cycle through careful discrimination. This means eliminating the unnecessary. There may be conflict between your creative desires and your sense of responsibility. Knowing how to prioritise is your key task right now.

30 Be more philosophical about aspects of your life that challenge you. It is only a matter of time before you remove them systematically to create a more satisfactory state of affairs.

31 Being rational today is not going to help. Rely on your intuition, and it will bring a surprise answer.

❊ SEPTEMBER ❊

Monthly Overview

Pressures ease, but you may feel somewhat flat and unmotivated up until the 5th. On the 6th, 13th, 19th and 20th you can look forward to some fun times, and perhaps even some romantic interludes.

1 You dislike people who grovel to the boss and think they can gain favours from being nice. Don't make enemies of them, though.

2 You need to adopt the good behaviour and work practices of those who are successful. By doing so, you will significantly increase your chance of success.

3 You like the idea of meeting aesthetically inclined people who can introduce you to new art forms and activities. But this means leaving lazier, less adventurous friends behind.

4 You'll surmount a problem today, and this will draw you closer to the ones you love. They may also feel a sense of relief in meeting you on common ground.

5   Your thinking is deep today, and you are not interested in superficiality. Because of this, others may not understand you. That's okay; you are allowed to be an enigma for the time being.

6   Friends or relatives may visit and bring sparkle to your domestic environment. This should be a loving and enjoyable day.

7   You may oscillate between two extreme opinions or courses of action. If this is the case, it is not the right time to make your final decision.

8   If you are appalled at the way things are proceeding, you need to hatch a new idea, even if others oppose it. Time will prove you to be correct.

9   There is something beautiful about disciplined, routine timetabling. Doing this frees you up to do truly creative things once the mundane tasks are finished. Work on your diary.

10   What you are expounding may fall on deaf ears. Don't throw pearls before swine.

11   If something is redundant, there is no point in hanging on to it. There are more efficient ways of doing things. This goes for people, too.

12 If you speculate, you need to be sure of what you are gambling on. If you trust another's word, you may lose.

13 You need to create a space that is sacrosanct where you can be yourself without anyone trespassing. Work on this today.

14 If you intervene in the disputes or negative affairs of others, you may end up getting the raw end of the deal, no matter how noble your intentions.

15 If you've been spending money on something that's draining your hard-earned cash, you need to put a stop to it. Redirect your funds.

16 You need to cover for someone else, but you'll feel uncomfortable in the process. Don't do this too often or it will wear your friendship thin.

17 Don't degrade yourself by grovelling for something. Hold your head up high and maintain your dignity.

18 Relocate if you are not comfortable where you are. I don't mean moving house. Relocate your office, chair or position, and it will reinvigorate your mind.

19 You may meet people who are well off, probably better off than you, but don't let this demean you or cause you to be dissatisfied with your lot. Remember, they have their own problems too.

20 If you've finished your work, you can attempt some sort of journey or holiday, but the operative word is 'if'. Planning a vacation is on the cards.

21 Altruism won't work today, and neither will it encourage others to do better. Today's key word is pragmatism.

22 If you could replicate yourself, there would be one of you sweeping the floors, one of you washing the dishes, one of you cooking and one of you sitting back watching your favourite soap opera. Unfortunately, this is not the case. It looks like it will be more of the same today.

23 You may be sad to hear news of someone who is not well or going through some personal tragedy. Send your best energy to them, pray, or call them to let them know that you support them.

24 Don't hedge your bets with one or more friends today. Be clear on your position, even if you run the risk of alienating them.

25 Your heritage will be important at present, and you may even be interested in understanding your family roots. Use this knowledge to secure a better life.

26 Make a bold statement for maximum impact, especially if you find yourself in a group or giving a presentation. What you have to share will go over well.

27 You may need to repudiate someone else's facts. If you have expertise in some area, it will come in handy today.

28 You need to take breaks to refresh your mind and rest your body. Mercury and Saturn create a slow and tedious pace.

29 It could be a case of mistaken identity, but you feel that someone resembles a friend or a long lost character in your life. This will bring back many memories.

30 Don't settle for mediocrity in affairs of the heart. You need to enforce your high standards at all times.

✦ OCTOBER ✦

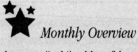

Monthly Overview

As a result of the Moon/Mars combination in your marital zone, harsh words, impulsive actions and a clash of wills are likely this month. Business partnerships can be antagonising, so keep a cool head and find conciliatory ways to address the issues. Brilliant, innovative and creative expression finds its way into your work activities, and you'll get good reactions from others between the 6th and the 10th.

---

1 There may be frustration over monetary matters.
   The cause is indiscriminate spending by a loved one.
   You need to take prompt action to stem the flow of cash.

---

2 No booklet on life is going to teach you how to adjust
   to the real-life challenges that arise. Trust in your own
   instincts to solve problems rather than relying on
   hand-me-down information.

---

3 Panic mode may set in, especially if you have
   misunderstood some directive by a co-worker or
   employer. Clarify the meaning and the intent.

---

4 Don't muddle your way through a situation, as a competitor may sense your ineptitude. Be honest about your lack of knowledge.

5 You may underestimate the demands upon you today. If you've taken your eye off the ball, there is no way you are going to score a goal.

6 You are not comfortable with doing menial work today, especially if it is by default or someone is slacking off. If you have done this in the past, you have no-one else to blame but yourself.

7 Someone's incompetence will rile you, but you have to understand that not everyone is as experienced or quick off the mark as you. You need to be compassionate and patient today.

8 You can settle scores in an amicable fashion during this cycle. Actually, you will realise that you've been a hard task master with someone and need to relax the discipline a little.

9 You are sweating over some information arriving, but you needn't. Distract yourself with other positive activities, and when the time is right, the news will arrive.

10 If you are missing one or two components of an equation, you are not going to find a solution today. You need to delve deeper before you get there.

11 Contracts, communications and other vital information could be at a crawling pace, much to your dissatisfaction. Don't waste too much time on this; start on something else.

12 Make a move if you have to, but preferably away from those who wish to control your life and the people in it. A growing sense of independence is looming.

13 Advertising your services is a good idea, but remember to study your demographic first.

14 Don't for a minute think that disagreements are a bad thing. It is just the way you approach them that counts. By understanding the differences between you and others, you can learn the art of compromise.

15 A friend may be far away, but this doesn't mean that you need to lose contact. Make an effort to call or email them today.

16 You need to repair and service vehicles or other mechanical equipment to keep them in good working order. Don't avoid your responsibilities or you will suffer an inevitable breakdown sooner or later.

17 Recycling may be on your mind as a way of saving money and helping the environment.

18 Supporting someone you love may be a time-consuming sacrifice on your part. But is it a sacrifice if you love doing it?

19 If you can't find clothes that fit or that are in keeping with your taste in fashion, perhaps you should visit a tailor and have something custom-made to your needs.

20 Take care of your joints, particularly your knees. There may be some problem associated with this area of your physiology, and it may have to do with excessive workouts, running or even faulty shoes.

21 Due to your exuberance, you may pay more for something than it is actually worth. Shop around and compare prices before reaching into your pockets.

22 The financial theme continues today, but let's extend that to your banking and financial needs. Seek out a better rate for your savings, and a reduced interest rate for your credit cards.

23 You have a need to connect with some campus or educational institution. This may be on behalf of someone else, but it will trigger your own interest in expanding your knowledge.

24 You have partly recovered from some minor illness and have a false sense of confidence. Allow your body to heal before pushing yourself to the limit again.

25 You need to act, but blind actions will cause problems. Think about what you want, visualise it, then act!

26 You may want the latest and greatest, but remember that new-release gadgets are the ones with the most problems. Take a step back and research any new device or object of desire.

27 Moderation is your key word today, but mostly in relation to your mental and emotional state. Don't overthink or overdramatise a situation.

28 Smile, even if you feel a little sad today. This will attract better circumstances. You'll find that things will turn around by sunset.

29 Remaining silent is not always a sign of weakness. In fact, it can endow you with considerable power. Remember, actions speak louder than words.

30 You may be dragging your feet today as a form of retaliation. Swallow your pride and spur yourself on.

31 Showing what you can do can make you feel more confident, but it can also be an example to others. You can shine as a leader today.

☀ NOVEMBER ☀

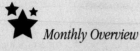

Monthly Overview

You can't control other people and their spending habits this month, so don't try to impose your will on them. There may be some unexpected financial complications around the 4th that will result in disputes. The same may occur after the 24th. You will be overloaded at work due to the Sun, Venus and Saturn in your zone of workplace activities, but this will also showcase your talents and give you a prime opportunity to move up the ladder of success.

---

1   You may be kidding about something today, only to find that someone has taken your words far more seriously than you expected. Remain sensitive to other people's feelings.

---

2   This is no time to resign, even if the going is getting tough. You have an obligation to yourself to work through the challenging times, which will make you feel stronger.

---

3 If you are wishing for something new in life, you need to back that up with careful planning, strong willpower and dynamic action. If one of these is missing, you lack the foundation for achieving your goals.

4 There is no harm in asking for proof if someone is trying to reel you in on a deal. No proof, no deal.

5 This is an intense interval, and you need to balance your expenditure with your income. Tighten the belt today.

6 Brushing up on basic skills, such as arithmetic, geometry and other long-forgotten formulas, may come in handy now. This is just a precaution.

7 How effective are you in your personal life? Are you fulfilled? You need to spot the holes in a relationship to patch them up.

8 You're being supported but don't recognise it. Stop beating yourself up. Take heed of someone's desire to help you enjoy life more.

9 If someone is asking you to do something, there will be conditions attached. If you are too generous, you will be making a rod for your own back.

10 The Moon enters your finance zone today, and you may expect a greater influx of wealth. You are a long way off from being rich, but think of ways to invest your money wisely to ensure a secure future.

11 You know that something will happen today, but don't pre-empt the outcome. Others need to go through certain processes for their own growth.

12 A sudden-death situation is nothing to be alarmed about. It simply means that you have to kill off an impending situation that could become harmful in the future. This is a wise move.

13 Family life can be unmanageable if you have no organisation in place. Focus on this today.

14 Remain upright in your dealings, even if someone else is not. If you resist their manipulations, there is less chance that they will try this in the future.

15 Rather than venturing outside your local area, seek out places and activities of interest in your vicinity.

16 There may be conflicts arising out of theological differences within your family. A single rule should prevail: respect for all.

17 You can mount a friendly assault on a competitor now, which will give you a distinctly unfair advantage in the marketplace.

18 You will appreciate just how stable you are at present. The more you think about it, the more stable you become. This is a consequence of the law of success.

19 Unless you accept that certain situations, people and relationships are transient, you'll be forever living in a world of 'what ifs'. Accept things as they are.

20 You're restricting your ability to grow and mature spiritually by staying with the tried and true. Today is a day of exploring new circumstances and people.

21 You could have a profound insight but may not be able to verbalise it. These inner understandings are for your wisdom only.

22 Don't be hasty in expressing some of your deeper, more loving feelings to a newcomer. You have more time than you think to deepen this relationship.

23 The New Moon in your marital zone brings a feeling of satisfaction and relevance. Your connections are very strong today.

24 You may have an interest in antiques or other unusual imports. Once again, it is a matter of selecting a store that doesn't add a premium on its price simply because it is in an upmarket area.

25 We usually need a map of the terrain we are exploring. Likewise, we need to understand our destination in life before we can embark on the journey. Beginning at the end is necessary sometimes.

26 Dancing is a great way to release pent-up tension and experience part of your spiritual nature. This should be a thoroughly enjoyable day, as long as you can let go a little.

27 You have greater resources than you think, but you haven't begun to tap them yet. Think about broadening your horizons and utilising what is available.

28 Your key word today is 'stop'. You are moving too quickly and errors may occur. When you were a child, you were told to look to the right, look to the left and look to the right again before crossing the road. The same applies to your interactions with others today.

29 Take care of your dental hygiene at present. The hard aspect of the Moon to Saturn in your sixth house of health indicates that there is some maintenance that needs to take place.

30 Be delicate with others who are suffering at the moment. Your advice can help them, but the way you dish out your truth is also important.

❄ DECEMBER ❄

Monthly Overview

Other people are your focus just now, and Saturn, Mercury, the Sun and Venus highlight how busy you will be with this task. The 6th to the 8th is telling, but after the 12th your communication issues ease. Wait until after the 24th to travel, if you must.

---

1 You've compartmentalised some activities that need integration. This will require some creativity and help from friends.

---

2 If you are trying to do some good deeds, make sure your assistance doesn't enable someone's bad behaviour. For example, don't donate money to a beggar who simply wants another bottle of wine!

---

3 You have influence and the power to do good today. But you need to put yourself out there to achieve this.

---

4 'Trust' is your key word during the next day or two. To gain the trust of others, exhibit your own trustworthiness.

5 Being original is not easy. Mimicking others and putting a spin on it is not enough. You need to meditate and go deep within yourself to dig up some gems of originality.

6 You may be in the headlines of your limited social circle, but you will quickly find that stealing the limelight is not all that it's cut out to be.

7 Neighbours could be bothering you. Or something in your immediate environment could be getting on your nerves, such as workmen, construction or even a natural phenomenon, like too many birds chirping at four o'clock in the morning.

8 If you are being sized up for a new position, remember that you need to size up the other person as well. It is a two-way street, so don't feel intimidated by those who seem larger than life.

9 If you know you are going to have a clash with someone, it is best to sidestep the situation. If you don't, your home will become a screaming mess and the result will be an extended stalemate.

10 An electrical or mechanical upgrade will be a surprise cost, but it is unavoidable. On that note, your power consumption may be up, so this is the time to cut back costs or 'go green'.

11 You're entitled to return things if they are not up to scratch. You mustn't allow embarrassment to get in the way of a just refund.

12 Someone's tactless behaviour could be grinding on your nerves. If this goes on for too long, you'll be forced to say something in a forceful manner.

13 You may be assigned a rather tedious task that will steal valuable time from your other projects. Look deeply into this as you may be able to learn something from the experience and apply it to other work.

14 Your partner's behaviour may be inexplicable today. There is no point trying to figure it out. Give them some space to work through their mood. In the meantime, reflect on your own state of mind. This will be helpful for both of you.

15 You need to reserve your attack for a more appropriate time, even if your impulses dictate otherwise. If you bide your time, you will be able to make a bolder and more effective statement.

16 No one can cramp your style today as the Moon and Mars indicate a strong drive to get mobile and physical. This is advisable.

17 Who says you have to put on a mandatory personality? You can be whoever you like, and my recommendation is that you explore some of your hidden personality traits. You are a Gemini, after all!

18 You may feel saddened by the manipulation of many by the few, but there is no point in whining or crying about this. Do something about it in a practical way.

19 A trial performance in some new career path or environment may make you feel nervous. The less you think about it, the more accomplished your performance will be.

20 Your imagination is creating problems that aren't there. If you must imagine, let it be positive, and this will continue to transform your relationships.

21 If you are modelling yourself after others, make sure those mentors and role models are beyond reproach. There is no harm in testing those you think are 'perfect'.

22 Frank Zappa once said that 'without deviation there is no progress'. This may sound like abstract philosophy, but there is a great deal of truth to it. Dare to be different.

23 Symbolic gestures often have a great impact on others. Today you may need to use this to send a distinct message to someone.

24 It's your choice how you tackle the festive season this year, but don't spread yourself thinly by saying yes to too many people.

25 Merry Christmas, Gemini! The Moon is in the upper part of your horoscope, indicating wonderful feelings of affection and love. Spread the feeling today for optimum results.

26 How you feel today is dependent on what you ate yesterday. Your moods are affected by your diet at present. Eat sparingly, if that is at all possible at Christmas.

27 There is no race to get back to work, so you will need to direct yourself into some fun activities and enjoy this festive season while it lasts.

28 You mustn't lose your cool if a friend lets you down. A change of plans may work out better in the end.

29 You will be guarded about sharing intimate secrets with someone who has never shared anything about him- or herself. This could create more distance between you, but so be it. Friendship has to be mutual.

30 You need to rest as the year comes to a close. Simplifying your life is the order of the day.

31 The last day of the year is a mixture of compulsion and struggle. Why do either? These pressures are created in your own mind. Look forward to the New Year.

2014
ASTRONUMEROLOGY

OUR DESTINY RULES OVER US, EVEN
WHEN WE ARE NOT YET AWARE OF IT;
IT IS THE FUTURE THAT MAKES LAWS
FOR OUR TODAY.

Friedrich Nietzsche

THE POWER BEHIND
❦ YOUR NAME ❦

Everything in nature is ruled by numbers, including your name and birthday. By simply adding up the numbers of your name, the vibration and ruling planet of this number can be calculated, and through that we can study the effects on your life and destiny. There is an ancient system of numerology that originated in Chaldea. It is somewhat different from the system devised by Pythagoras, but it is equally, if not more, powerful and takes into account the planets and the effects on your name and birthday. Here is a table of the letters, numbers and ruling planets associated with them.

AIJQY	=	1	Sun
BKR	=	2	Moon
CGLS	=	3	Jupiter
DMT	=	4	Uranus
EHNX	=	5	Mercury
UVW	=	6	Venus
OZ	=	7	Neptune
FP	=	8	Saturn
—	=	9	Mars

Note: The number 9 is a spiritual number and, according to the ancient tradition of Chaldean numerology, is not assigned a letter. It is considered an unknowable number. Once the name or birthday numbers have been calculated, the number 9 is used as a sum total number for interpretation.

Throughout history, many people have changed their names for good luck, including actors, writers and musicians. They have done this in the hope of attracting good fortune by using the numbers of the planets connected with that birth date. If you look at the following table of numbers and their meanings, you will have a greater insight into how you can change your name and use this to your own advantage for more fulfilling relationships, wealth, general happiness and success.

Here is an example of how you can calculate the number and power of your name. If your name is Barack Obama, you can calculate the ruling numbers as follows:

B	A	R	A	C	K		O	B	A	M	A
2	1	2	1	3	2		7	2	1	4	1

Now add the numbers like this:

$2 + 1 + 2 + 1 + 3 + 2 + 7 + 2 + 1 + 4 + 1$ = 26

Then add $2 + 6$ = 8

You can now see that the sum total of the numbers is 8, which is ruled by Saturn, and that the underlying vibrations of 2 and 6 are ruled by the Moon and Venus. You can now study the Name Number table to see what these planetary energies and numbers mean for Barack Obama. We can see from Saturn that he is an extremely hard-working and ambitious person with incredible concentration and the ability to sacrifice a lot for his chosen objectives. From Venus and the Moon, we see that he is a person possessing a delightful, charming and persuasive personality, and that he has a strong love for his family.

Name Number	Ruling Planet	Name Characteristics
1	Sun	Being ruled by the Sun means you possess abundant energy and attract others with your powerful aura. You are bright, magnetic and attractive as well. You are generous and loyal in disposition. Because of your high levels of energy, you need sport to make you feel good. You succeed in any enterprise you choose.
2	Moon	You are emotional and your temperament is soft and dreamy, but you must be careful of extreme mood swings. You are psychic and can use your intuitive hunches to understand others and gain an insight into your future. You have strong connections to your mother, family and women in general. Your caring and compassionate nature will make you popular with others.

Name Number	Ruling Planet	Name Characteristics
3	Jupiter	You seem to attract good luck without too much effort, but you must be on guard as you are likely to be excessive even when you are generous. You have strong philosophical instincts and wish to understand why you are here. Travelling is high on your agenda and you will explore many different facets of life and culture. You are a perennial student who wants to learn more about yourself and life in general.
4	Uranus	The number 4 is an unpredictable number, so you need to plan adequately for your life. It will have many unforeseen twists and turns, but you are extra-ordinarily innovative in the way you deal with life issues. You need unusual friends as you get bored easily, and it's quite likely you will take an interest in techno-logical or scientific things. Learning to be flexible will go a long way in helping you secure a happy and fulfilling life.

Name Number	Ruling Planet	Name Characteristics
5	Mercury	Speed and accuracy are the key words for the planet Mercury and the number 5. You love communication and connect with people easily, but you need to be on guard against dissipating your energies into many frivolous activities. This is a youthful number, and you never grow old. You will always be surrounded by youngsters and people who make you laugh. You have a great sense of humour and will always be successful as you have the gift of the gab.
6	Venus	You have a natural inclination to love and be loved if you are ruled by the number 6 and Venus. Having a delightful personality, you attract many people of the opposite sex. You are successful with money and take great pleasure in working towards your future security. You will have many love affairs, and at some point you may even be torn between two lovers.

Name Number	Ruling Planet	Name Characteristics
7	Neptune	With the number 7 as your ruling number, you have reached a very high level of evolution. You are gifted with premonitions, intuition and clairvoyance. Health and healing are also gifts that you have been endowed with. Learn to discriminate when giving yourself to others.
8	Saturn	You have incredible focus and an ability to achieve anything you set your mind to, no matter how long it takes. You sacrifice for others as your loyalty is highly developed. You work hard to achieve things you believe are worthwhile, but sometimes this overshadows your personal life. You demand that things are done properly, which is why others may not be able to live up to your expectations. Learn to relax a little more.
9	Mars	You have a hot nature and need an outlet such as sport and other physical activities to balance your life and improve your health. You are not afraid of challenges and can be confrontational. Learn to listen and accept that others don't have the same attitudes as you. You are a protector of the family and loyal to the core. You are an individual and never follow another's lead.

YOUR PLANETARY
❧ RULER ❧

Numerology is intimately linked to the planets, which is why astrology and your date of birth are also spiritually connected. Once again, here are the planets and their ruling numbers:

1   Sun

2   Moon

3   Jupiter

4   Uranus

5   Mercury

6   Venus

7   Neptune

8   Saturn

9   Mars

Finding your birth numbers is simple. All you have to do is add each of the numbers of your date of birth to arrive at a single digit number. If you're born on 12 November 1972, add the numbers of your day, month and year of birth to find your destiny number, like this:

$1 + 2 + 1 + 1 + 1 + 9 + 7 + 2 = 24$

Then add $\qquad 2 + 4 = 6$

This means that the number 6, which is ruled by Venus, is your destiny number.

YOUR PLANETARY
✦ FORECAST ✦

You can even take your ruling name number and add it to the year in question to throw more light on your coming personal affairs, like this:

B A R A C K O B A M A	=	8
Year coming	=	2014
Add 8 + 2 + 0 + 1 + 4	=	15
Add 1 + 5	=	6

This is the ruling year number using your name number as a basis. Therefore, you would study the influence of Venus (number 6) using the Trends for Your Planetary Ruler in 2014 table. Enjoy!

Trends for Your Planetary Number in 2014

Year Number	Ruling Planet	Results Throughout the Coming Year
1	Sun	

Overview

You are now ready to move forward in a new cycle and create something wonderful for yourself and your loved ones. Your career, finance and personal reputation will improve considerably and your physical health should also be much better. Although there may be some challenges, you're able to meet them head-on and come out a winner.

Love and Pleasure

You can attract anyone you want throughout 2014 because your energy and aura are so strong. You will need many friends and will find yourself doing creative activities alone and with others.

Work

You will have no problem getting a better job or some sort of promotion in your current line of work. More money can be expected, and any changes you make in your life should bring you great satisfaction.

Improving Your Luck

Good luck is on the cards, with July and August being especially lucky for you. The 1st, 8th, 15th and 22nd hours of Sundays are lucky.

Lucky numbers are 1, 10, 19 and 28.

Year Number	Ruling Planet	Results Throughout the Coming Year
2	Moon	

Overview

Although you will feel emotional this year, it's time to take control of yourself and change your personality for the better. Working through issues with females, both at home and in the workplace, may be the key to your happiness and success this year.

Love and Pleasure

Domestic affairs and relationships at home will take centre stage in 2014. Your marital relationship or important significant friendships are high on your agenda of things to improve. You are sensitive and intuitive, so trust your gut feeling when it comes to making decisions in this area of your life.

Work

Make your decisions based on rational thought rather than impulsive emotional reactions. Draw a clear line in the sand between work and leisure for best results. You are more creative this year, so hopefully you will take the opportunity to move along that path rather than doing something you are bored with.

Year Number	Ruling Planet	Results Throughout the Coming Year
2	Moon	**Improving Your Luck**

Mondays will be lucky and July will fulfill some of your dreams. The 1st, 8th, 15th and 22nd hours on Mondays are fortunate. Pay special attention to the New and Full Moons in 2014.

Lucky numbers are 2, 11, 20, 29 and 38.

Year Number	Ruling Planet	Results Throughout the Coming Year
3	Jupiter	

Overview

A number 3 year is usually a lucky one due to the beneficial influence of Jupiter. New opportunities, financial good fortune, travels and spiritual insights will be key factors in the coming year.

Love and Pleasure

You have a huge appetite for love, and bond easily with others to fulfil this need. Try to clarify your feelings before investing too much energy into someone who may not be the best choice. This is a year of entertainment and pleasure, and one in which generosity will bring good karma to you.

Work

You can finally ask for that pay rise as this is a lucky year when money will naturally come to you. Promotions, interviews for a new position and general good fortune can be expected.

Improving Your Luck

Don't let harebrained schemes distract you from the practical aspects of life. Good planning is necessary for success. March and December are lucky months. 2014 will bring you some unexpected surprises. The 1st, 8th, 15th and 24th hours of Thursdays are spiritually very lucky for you.

Lucky numbers are 3, 12, 21, and 30.

Year Number	Ruling Planet	Results Throughout the Coming Year
4	Uranus	

Overview

Expect the unexpected with this ruling number for the coming year. If you have spread yourself thinly, then you may lack the requisite energy to handle the changes that are coming. Independence is your key word, but impulse is also likely. Take your time before making important decisions, and structure your life appropriately.

Love and Pleasure

The grass may not be greener on the other side, and if you're feeling trapped in a relationship, you will want to break free of the entanglements that are strangling your self-development. You need to balance tradition with progress if you are to come out of this period a happy person.

Work

Innovation will help you make good progress in your professional life. Learn something new, especially in the technological arena. If you have been reluctant to improve your skill set, you are shooting yourself in the foot. Expand your horizons, learn new tasks and improve your professional future. Group activity will also help you carve a new niche for yourself.

Year Number	Ruling Planet	Results Throughout the Coming Year
4	Uranus	**Improving Your Luck**

Try not to overdo things this year, and learn to be more forbearing with others. Slow and steady wins the race in 2014. Steady investments are lucky. The 1st, 8th, 15th and 20th hours of Saturdays will be very lucky for you.

Lucky numbers are 4, 13, 22 and 31.

Year Number	Ruling Planet	Results Throughout the Coming Year
5	Mercury	

Overview

You want to socialise and communicate your feelings this year because you have such a creative and powerful imagination, and it is likely you will connect with many new people. Try not to spread yourself too thinly, as concentration levels may be lacking. Don't be distracted by the wrong crowd.

Love and Pleasure

Reciprocation is important for your relationships in 2014. Variety is the spice of life, but also ensure that your key partnership will weather the storm and get stronger with time. Talk about your feelings, even if this is difficult. Don't be too harsh and critical of the one you love; instead, turn the spotlight of criticism on yourself to improve your character.

Work

People will look up to you in the coming 12 months, which is why new contracts will be drawn and doors will open to provide you with a bright new professional future. You are quick and capable, but try not to overdo things, as this can affect your nervous system. Travel is a great way to balance these energies.

Year Number	Ruling Planet	Results Throughout the Coming Year
5	Mercury	**Improving Your Luck**

Expressing ideas is essential and it will help you come up with great plans that others want to help you with. By being enthusiastic and creative, you will attract the support of those who count. The 1st, 8th, 15th and 20th hours of Wednesdays are your luckiest, so schedule your meetings and other important social engagements at these times.

Lucky numbers are 5, 14, 23 and 32.

Year Number	Ruling Planet	Results Throughout the Coming Year
6	Venus	

Overview

A year of love. Expect romantic and sensual interludes or a new love affair. Number 6 is also related to family life. Working with a loved one or family member is possible, and it will yield good results. Save money, cut costs and share your success.

Love and Pleasure

Love will be important to you, and if you are in a relationship, you can strengthen the bonds with your partner at this time. Making new friends is also on the cards, and these relationships will become equally significant, especially if you are not yet hitched. Engagement, marriage and other important celebrations take place. You will find yourself more socially active.

Work

You have a desire to work on your future financial security, so cutting back costs would be a key factor in this. You may find yourself with more money, but don't let false illusions cause you to spend more than you earn. Developing your part-time interest into a fully-fledged career is also something that can take place this year. Your social life and professional activities will overlap.

Year Number	Ruling Planet	Results Throughout the Coming Year
6	Venus	**Improving Your Luck**

Developing a positive mental attitude will attract good luck and karma that is now ripe for the picking. Enjoy your success, but continue to work on removing those personality defects that are obstructing you from even bigger success. Balance spiritual and financial needs. The 1st, 8th, 15th and 20th hours on Fridays are extremely lucky for you this year, and new opportunities can arise when you least expect them.

Lucky numbers are 6, 15, 24 and 33.

Year Number	Ruling Planet	Results Throughout the Coming Year
7	Neptune	

Overview

You have the power to intuitively understand what needs to be done in 2014. Trust your instincts and make greater efforts at your spiritual and philosophical wellbeing. This is the time when your purpose becomes crystal clear. You can gain a greater understanding of yourself and others and have the ability to heal those who need your help both within and outside your family.

Love and Pleasure

If you can overcome the tendency to find fault with yourself, you will start to truly love yourself and attract those who also love you. This is the key law of success in love, and you will discover this in the coming 12 months. Don't give more than others are prepared to reciprocate. You need to set your standards high enough to meet someone who is worthy of your love.

Work

This is the year to stop watching the clock and produce incredibly wonderful work. No matter how menial the task, you can experience the spiritual significance of work and how this can be used to uplift others. The healing, caring and social services professions may attract you just now.

Year Number	Ruling Planet	Results Throughout the Coming Year
7	Neptune	**Improving Your Luck**

Improving Your Luck

Be clear in your communication so as to avoid misunderstandings with others. If you have some health issues, now is the time to clear them up and improve your general vitality. Sleep well, exercise and develop better eating habits to improve your life. The 1st, 8th, 15th and 20th hours of Wednesdays are your luckiest, so schedule your meetings and other important social engagements at these times.

Lucky numbers are 7, 16, 25 and 34.

Year Number	Ruling Planet	Results Throughout the Coming Year
8	Saturn	

Overview

This is a year of achievement, but it will require discipline and a removal of all distractions to achieve your goals. Eliminating unnecessary aspects of your life that constrict your success will be something you need to pay attention to. Your overall success may be slow, but it is assured.

Love and Pleasure

By overworking, you deny your loved ones the pleasure of your company and emotional support. Take the time to express how you feel. Remember that love is a verb. Spend more time with your loved ones as a countermeasure to excessive work routines.

Work

This is a money year, and the Chinese will tell you that the number 8 is very lucky indeed. But remember that money can't buy you love. Earn well, but also learn to balance your income potential with creative satisfaction.

Year Number	Ruling Planet	Results Throughout the Coming Year
8	Saturn	**Improving Your Luck**

Improving Your Luck

If you are too cautious you may miss wonderful opportunities. Of course, you don't want to make mistakes, but sometimes these mistakes are the best lessons that life can dish out. Have courage and don't be afraid to try something new. The 1st, 8th, 15th and 20th hours of Saturdays are the best times for you in 2014.

Lucky numbers are 1, 8, 17, 26 and 35.

Year Number	Ruling Planet	Results Throughout the Coming Year
9	Mars	

Overview

This is the last cycle, which means that you will be tying up loose ends over the coming 12 months. Don't get caught up in trivial matters as this is the perfect time to redirect your energy into what you want in life. Don't be angry, avoid arguments and clearly focus on what you want now.

Love and Pleasure

You want someone who can return the love, energy and passion that you have for them. If this isn't happening, you may choose to end a relationship and find someone new. Even if you need to transition to a new life, try to do this with grace and diplomacy.

Work

You can be successful this year because of the sheer energy you are capable of investing into your projects. Finish off what is incomplete as there are big things around the corner, and you don't want to leave a mess behind. You can obtain respect and honour from your employers and co-workers.

Year Number	Ruling Planet	Results Throughout the Coming Year

Improving Your Luck

Don't waste your valuable energy this year. Use it to discover the many talents that you possess. By doing this you can begin to improve your life in many different ways. Release tension to maintain health. The 1st, 8th, 15th and 20th hours of Tuesdays will be lucky for you throughout 2014.

Lucky numbers are 9, 18, 27 and 36.

The World of Mills & Boon®

There's a Mills & Boon® series that's perfect for you. We publish ten series and, with new titles every month, you never have to wait long for your favourite to come along.

Blaze®

Scorching hot, sexy reads
4 new stories every month

By Request

Relive the romance with the best of the best
9 new stories every month

Cherish™

Romance to melt the heart every time
12 new stories every month

Desire™

Passionate and dramatic love stories
8 new stories every month